CONNECTICU

TAKEN

D1236427

THOMAS R. BAYLES
LOCAL HISTORY
COLLECTION

Donated by Davis Erhardt

Longwood Public Library
Middle Island, NY

PECONIC BAY

GREAT

BAY

SOUTH

OCEAN

AT

THE "GOLD COAST"

DYNAMICS OF COMMUNITY CHANGE

DENNIS P. SOBIN

IRA J. FRIEDMAN, INC. / PORT WASHINGTON, N.Y. 1968

DYNAMICS OF COMMUNITY CHANGE

The Case of Long Island's Declining "Gold Coast"

TITLE PAGE ILLUSTRATION

The Syosset-Muttontown area clearly showing the side-by-side existence of old country estates and new small-home developments on Long Island's "Gold Coast." (photo courtesy of Lockwood, Kessler, and Bartlett, Inc. Consulting Engineers.)

ACKNOWLEDGEMENTS

To the University of Illinois Press for permission to reproduce the chart that appears on page 19, originally published in *Urban Land Use Planning* 2nd edition, by F. Stuart Chapin (1965), p. 64.

To McGraw-Hill Publications for permission to reprint excerpts that appear on pages 43, 44, and 46, originally published in the *Architectural Record* (December, 1904), p. 532, and the *Architectural Record* (March, 1921), p. 224.

To Charles Scribner's Sons for permission to reprint excerpts that appear on pages 71 and 72, originally published in *The Great Gatsby* by F. Scott Fitzgerald (1925), pp. 39-41.

DYNAMICS OF COMMUNITY CHANGE

Copyright © 1968 by Dennis P. Sobin
All Rights Reserved
Library of Congress Catalog Card No. 68-8249
Manufactured in the United States of America

EMPIRE STATE HISTORICAL PUBLICATIONS SERIES 59
Published and distributed by
Ira J. Friedman, Inc.
Port Washington, N.Y., 11050

LONGWOOD PUBLIC LIBRARY

To Paulette,
My Very Capable Secretary,
Critic, Research Assistant,
and Wife

Preface

A study of community change, involving as it does an analysis of complex relationships among people and dynamic forces, never is an easy task. When the community being investigated happens to be one with a reputation for being highly exclusive and protective, such a study becomes formidable, indeed.

I relate this not as an exercise in self-exaltation but as an explanation for my heavy reliance upon many persons who aided me in my research. Their help I gratefully acknowledge.

A complete list of those who contributed in various degrees to this work would be exceedingly lengthy; nor could it be complete. Several hundred persons were interviewed and volunteered valuable information. A few, moreover, have requested that their anonymity be preserved.

Among the more important contributors were present-day millionaire estate owners and decendents of former estate owners. These persons were extremely generous in time spent and knowledge conveyed. Other interviews which were of immense value were conducted with local public officials and community leaders.

My many sessions with estate superintendents and other estate employees, both active and retired, were highly productive.

These informants were very knowledgeable and articulate in their Gold Coast commentary. Finally, the numerous local historians and librarians with whom conferences were held provided many leads to significant sources of information.

In addition to those persons who cooperated and contributed in the information-gathering stage of the project, many friends and colleagues must be counted as having provided ideas used in the planning of strategy and in the final analysis. Those deserving of particular recognition for their advice and guidance are John Calbreath Burdis (Nassau County Planning Commission); Richard R. Gardner (U.S. Economic Development Administration); Lee E. Koppelman (Nassau-Suffolk Regional Planning Board); Howard S. Quinn (New York State Office of Planning Coordination); and the late Stanley B. Tankel (Regional Plan Association).

Equally notable direction and encouragement were given by professors and colleagues at colleges with which I have been affiliated, both as student and lecturer. I would especially like to thank Doctors William M. Dobriner, Hyman A. Enzer, Robert A. Davison, and Dennis H. Wrong. Dr. Dobriner's own published work in the field of urban studies was itself a source of important information and inspiration.

Finally, to Cornell Jaray, a patient and prudent publisher, and to Peter Inserra, a polished and precise editor, I express my sincere appreciation.

D.P.S.

Contents

Part Two
THE DECLINE: AN INTERPRETATION

Part Three
CONCLUSION

Tables

Illustrations

DYNAMICS OF COMMUNITY CHANGE

1

Background and Approach

In a very real sense, the writer writes in order to teach himself, to understand himself, to satisfy himself; the publishing of his ideas, though it brings gratifications, is a curious anticlimax.

Alfred Kazin

This is a study of change, a narration and an interpretation. The change happened in a place with a distinctive physical and social character. Multi-million dollar estates were typical homes in this locale and here the world's wealthiest people lavishly lived and entertained. The area, early in this century, was called a Gold Coast.

These distinguishing characteristics have been disappearing over the years, and this process of change is continuing. It has caused many observers to question whether there is, indeed, a Gold Coast left.

This study has two objectives. The first is to describe the change that has taken place and the second, and more difficult, is to explain it.

3

THE SETTING

The study location is the traditional estate area on the North Shore of western Long Island along the Long Island Sound. This area forms a corridor twenty miles long with a width ranging from less than one mile at each end to about ten miles at the middle.

This land extends east from the New York City boundary, through all of northern Nassau County, to a point about four miles into the very northerly part of Suffolk County. It encompasses close to 50 small localities, most of them incorporated villages. This area amounts to about 110 square miles — just under ten per cent of all of Long Island.

The 110-square-mile area covers the northern part of Nassau County and the northwestern part of Suffolk County. Portions of three townships fall into this area. These are North Hempstead and Oyster Bay in Nassau County and Huntington in Suffolk County. Finally, there are twenty-five villages within its boundary.

This land has many fine natural characteristics. Its frontage on the deep Long Island Sound leading to the Atlantic Ocean and its many harbors and coves are its most prominent features. Its gently rolling hills are another attractive feature.

It was in the first two decades of this century that this land was developed into estates by the wealthy. By the end of the period, 600 estates existed in the area, located one after another in a virtually unbroken sequence. Most of the estates were over 50 acres in size and about 150 of them exceeded 100 acres. The expansive and expensive mansions of each estate contained upwards of 100 rooms and 30 baths.

During this time, the nation turned to the North Shore with excitement and envy. It saw great homes larger than hotels and much more costly built high on hills, some man-made for the purpose. It saw the extravagant parties given for the world's famous. It watched the greatest performers of the time privately entertain. And it read an enthralling novel by F. Scott Fitzgerald unmistakenly using its people and places.

Since that time, a major portion of the estate land has been developed and most of the multi-millionaires are gone. Though the area is still exclusive and prestigious by suburban standards, it no longer captures the nation's eye nor the novelist's imagination.

PURPOSE OF THE STUDY

It will be the initial task of this book to show how, when and to what extent the North Shore of Long Island became a Gold Coast. The narrative will then continue to the present, tracing the developments which appear to be symptomatic of the change that the North Shore has been experiencing.

Part I, "Gold Coast Development and Decline: A Narrative," will consider the transition of a homogeneous, tightly-knit, highly-restricted area into one reduced and fragmented. Only isolated sections of the North Shore, at best, have retained the features which once marked the entire area. Some observers maintain that the change on the North Shore has been no more than moderate. Most feel that it has been substantial, with far-reaching implications. Our evidence would clearly support this latter view.

This first part gives important background information and more significantly, provides the reader with an account of the considerable change — the decline of the Gold Coast over the last few decades. This is done to avoid the criticism that could be directed at Cleveland Amory's book, *Who Killed Society?* Mr. Amory begins his book with a search for the killers, overlooking the question of whether a death has actually occurred. Certainly his first job should have been to establish the death as fact. Attempting to benefit from his oversight, this study will not arrive at causes of the decline of the Gold Coast until it is demonstrated that this decline has really taken place. This will be done by contrasting the social and physical characteristics of the North Shore in its early history as an estate community to its present features.

Having substantiated the decline of Long Island's Gold Coast, this phenomenon will be explained. The objective will be to provide alternate explanations which will focus upon different factors. In one explanation, political factors will be the concern; in another, economic variables will be at issue; in a third, sociological factors will be considered; and the last explanation will focus on psychological considerations. It is hoped that in this way the importance of each set of variables will be recognized.

In a later section of this introductory chapter, various theories of community change will be critically reviewed so that the approach of this study can be set in a context with them. Before coming to this, an historical sketch of America's upper class will be presented. The background of this social group is an important consideration in a study of this kind. For the North Shore served as a haven for members of this class in the period when the Gold Coast flourished.

AN HISTORICAL SKETCH OF AMERICA'S UPPER CLASS

An upper class has existed in America in every period of history since colonial times. But its characteristics and functions have not always been the same. Even the name by which it is known varies. Though "upper class" seems to be the most common, other names used are "society" (Amory), "elite" (C. W. Mills), "aristocracy" (Baltzell), and "upper-upper class" (Warner). All these labels refer to that small segment of the population that is regarded by all of society, including itself, as occupying the uppermost level of the social strata.

The people who comprise the upper class have usually been those with the most social prestige, economic strength, and political power in society. These attributes are interrelated and are often found hand-in-hand with one another.

Over the years, the characteristics of the upper class have varied, but the most enduring characteristic has been possession of substantial wealth and/or a very high income. In the period since the Civil War, a good education and a highly respectable occupation have been relatively standard characteristics. In the early years of this country, an upper-class characteristic was the ownership of much land.

The first settlers to come to America were mostly people of the middle and lower classes in the country of their origin. As Dixon Wecter states: "The aristocrat whose birth and heritage gave him a stake in the old order had no reason for uprooting himself." The few persons of upper social rank who did come to this continent came as colonial governors, or in search of riches or adventure. Almost all of these, including the governors, returned to their homeland after their missions were over.

Nevertheless, an upper class, predominantly ingrown, did emerge in the colonial period. Since the earliest criterion of high social position became land ownership, many an early colonist competed for the acquisition of large tracts of land. Thomas Smith and Nicholas Bayard were among those who became great landowners.

By the eve of the Revolutionary War, America was characterized by class distinctions based on the distribution of property. A study of land distribution at this time in the Boston area has revealed that "property was concentrated in the hands of these rich men just as was the wealth of commercial farm areas: Boston's richest ten per cent had fifty-seven per cent of the wealth." [2]

The display of wealth has always been a means of reinforcing, if not establishing, social position. Though in the earliest part of this period opulence was just barely a characteristic of the upper class, extravagance became increasingly widespread and competitive. In the twenty-five year span between 1740 and 1765 it reached its peak. This period is described by Wecter as follows: "The quarter-century from 1740 to 1765 saw the greatest florescence of luxury which this land has ever known — silks, jewels, gold and silver plate, French and Spanish wines, portrait painting, carriages from London, horse-racing for high stakes, hunts, concerts, balls and plays...." [3] The writer maintains that this era compares to the Gilded Age in the three decades before World War I, the period when Long Island's

Gold Coast emerged.

Regional differences which were apparent among the colonial upper class should therefore be pointed out. The upper class most celebrated for elegance in dress, speech, dining, and sport was located in the South, primarily in Virginia and the Carolinas. These persons owned large plantations and resided in exquisite mansions. Here, strong connection between social rank and property ownership was especially evident. In the Carolinas after 1663, titles of nobility were issued by the government on the basis of land ownership. The title of "Baron" was given to persons who owned 12,000 acres, "Cacique" was for owners of 24,000 acres, and the top rank of "Landgrave" was reserved for owners of 48,000 acres.

Extensive land ownership for upper class members was somewhat less important in New England. Since trade and commerce played a primary role in the economy here, some of the most prominent citizens were merchants. In New England it was important not only that a person had wealth, but also how he came to acquire it. In accordance with Puritan beliefs of predestination, a person of lowly birth who acquired substantial wealth through intelligence, thrift, and industry was held to be divinely favored. It was considered impious to refuse him a high social place.

The third major region with an upper class was New York. Here, as in the South, land ownership was an important mark of an upper-class person. Landlord owners were designated "Patroons" and were entitled to the rights of lordship. Kiliaen Van Rensselaer, an early "Patroon," was the owner of a tract of some 700,000 acres along the west bank of the Hudson in 1630.

The upper class of both New England and New York seemed far less concerned with material display than that of the South. It has been said of New York, for example, that "the simplicity of life in colonial New York made ostentation almost impossible, though keeping one's own carriage was the notable badge of social plutocracy."[4] But the social unpretentiousness of the North was not destined to last. In the case of New York, the end came in the later eighteenth century when New York City temporarily served as the national seat of Government. "Its brief regime as the national capital, and its enduring status as the national metropolis, attracted rich and sophisticated visitors from the South, England, and the Continent."[5]

The American Revolution had an important impact on the upper class. Many of the wealthy and socially prominent opposed the revolutionary movement and supported the Loyalist cause. These persons sought to retain the old order under which they had prospered. When the war was over, many of these persons were sent to England while those who remained in America were awarded a much reduced social and economic standing.

Besides casting individuals out of the upper class, the war added new persons to it. The new members were the revolutionary leaders and statesmen.

Another result of the war was a shift in wealth accumulations. Merchants, supplying both sides with the materials of war, became wealthy, while incomes based on permanent investments, such as mortgages, dropped.

But the greatest effect of the war on the American upper class was brought about by changes in the value system. Embodied in the Declaration of Independence, the new values emphasized democratic principles and the equality of men.

According to Wecter, America strived to achieve the ideal of the Declaration of Independence in the first half of the nineteenth century. As a result, the ostentatious display of wealth was generally frowned upon and, therefore, was not practiced by the upper class.

In addition to the national feeling of egalitarianism placing a damper on upper-class extravagance, the level of affluence of the upper class in this period was not very high. Mills states:

> Before the Civil War, only a handful of wealthy men, notably Astor and Vanderbilt, were multimillionaires on a truly American scale. Few of the great fortunes exceeded $1,000,000. In fact, George Washington, who in 1799 left an estate valued at $530,000, was judged to be

one of the richest Americans of his time. By the 1840's in New York City and all of Massachusetts, there were only thirty-nine millionaires. The word "millionaire," in fact, was coined only in 1843, when, upon the death of Peter Lorillard (snuff, banking, real estate), the newspapers needed a term to denote great affluence.[6]

The composition and characteristics of the upper class were altered by the Civil War. Throughout the North, the war brought about a period of substantial money-making and lavish spending. As in all wars, military supplies were in great demand and the small industrial enterprises of the North were in an excellent position to expand and supply them. Many small industrialists were exceedingly wealthy men before the war's end.

The many opera houses, theatres, luxury hotels, and brownstone mansions that were built in the North during this period reflect the new wealth of the upper class. The North also saw such upper-class social events as formal balls and extravagant parties.

The upper class in the South, however, suffered a setback as a result of the war. Because of the tremendous strain the South was under to provide the materials of war, much of the Southern wealth was drained. The war also brought about a good deal of physical ruin of upper-class property in the South. Sherman's notorious march through the South caused the destruction of many elegant mansions.

After the war, the industrial revolution in America got under way. Fortunes were soon made in railroads, banking, oil, mining, and numerous other fields. The greatest wealth was probably derived from oil. Wecter states that "no phase of American industry has yielded a more spectacular harvest of fortunes than Standard Oil."[7]

Most of America's great fortunes of today had their origin in this period of great industrial expansion. This is true for the wealth of many present upper-class families who can trace their ancestry back to colonial times. The really big money came to these families in the late nineteenth century. Taking note of this, Wecter states that "a few families in the United States have long and excellent pedigrees, of which only a small segment is plated with gold."[8]

The majority of individuals who accumulated great wealth in the decades after the Civil War had very humble family backgrounds. Many were immigrants. The established upper class of the period realized that their ranks were being infiltrated by the new rich. An upper-class member has written that "all at once Society was assailed from every side by persons who sought to climb boldly over the walls of social exclusiveness."[9] A tighter organization of the upper class and a means of differentiating between upper-class and wealthy persons were necessary. As Mills' writes: "The extravagant wealth of the post-Civil War period called for a more articulate means of determining the elect."[10]

Ward McAllister, a close observer though not a full member of the upper class, offered various means of solidifying the upper class. He helped to organize great social affairs with guest lists of carefully screened individuals. In 1873, he named the "Patriarchs," a committee of twenty-five men designated as the leaders of the upper class. McAllister released a highly-publicized list in 1892 that contained the names of 400 people whom he held to be the core of the upper class.

Although McAllister's list was the first official roll of "Society" to be published, there is an earlier list similar to it which was prepared a century before. This is a "Dinner and Supper List for 1787 and 1788" of Mrs. John Jay, wife of the Secretary of Foreign Affairs, when New York was the national capital. A comparison of the two lists reveals changing characteristics of the upper-class core.

After comparing the two lists Wecter concludes that "the removal of the national capital from New York in 1889 decreed that its future 'Society,' unlike that of London, Paris, Rome, Berlin, Vienna, and other great cities, should be divorced from statesmanship. Political careers henceforth would not parallel social ones in the metropolitan pattern, which was to become increasingly gilt-edged, and perhaps more clannish, frivolous and indolent than a society interwoven with public service." [11] There are about the same number of lawyers in the first list as in the second, bankers have multiplied, several physicians in the first have dwindled to just one in the second, and clergymen are not present at all in the second.

Shortly after McAllister published his list, he lost his hold as a leader of the upper class. For, as he tried to preserve the "Old Guard," he made himself an enemy of the New Wealth, some of whose representatives had already become firmly established in the upper class.

Because of the growing strength and perseverance of the new rich to enter the upper class, Mills maintains that "the only sensible thing that could be done was to admit the new wealth, or at least selected members of it." [12] This, he claims, is what the *Social Register* has successfully attempted to do.

The first *Social Register* appeared in New York, Boston, and Philadelphia in 1890. By 1928, it was being published for twelve cities including Baltimore (1892), Chicago (1893), Buffalo (1903), Pittsburgh (1904), San Francisco (1906), Cleveland (1910), and Cincinnati (1910).

The appearance of one's name in the social register soon became a mark of upper-class membership. The names of the old-line upper class were automatically included in the book. The new rich had to become well known before their names would be entered. This was done by successfully playing the "social game," which is a competition among wealthy individuals for maximum social recognition. One attempts, for example, to have his name mentioned in the society pages as much as possible. The story is told of Harry Lehr, a participant in the social game in the late 19th century, who "sent a bruised flower to a hospital by special ambulance, and by a score of increasingly outrageous pranks made excellent copy for the press." [13] The society page became an important vehicle for upward social mobility.

Being invited to affairs sponsored by well-established socialites was also important to those who played the social game. Another concern was with owning certain commodities to serve as status markers. These included special types of clothing, perfumes, furs, automobiles, and homes.

In the 1920's, another upper-class list appeared. This was created by Maury Paul, a leading observer of the upper class. The list was divided into two columns titled "Old Guard" and "Cafe." The "Old Guard" was described as the sector of the upper class that adhered closely to upper-class traditions. "Cafe Society" was made up of upper-class persons who were not averse to adopting new ways.

The trends in upper-class composition and outlook that began in various periods after the Civil War have largely continued to the present. The distinction between "Cafe Society" and "Old Guard" is still in vogue. Also used today is the social register that is being published annually in many cities.

E. Digby Baltzell, a student of the contemporary upper class, has studied the present significance of the social register. He concludes that it is "a listing of families of high social class position." He distinguishes this group, the upper class, from the elite, which consists of "individuals of high functional class position." Though some individuals today belong to both groups, he claims that the groups are largely composed of different people.

The upper class of today differs somewhat in life style from the upper class of earlier periods. This is largely due to technological change which has occurred. Many improvements in transportation, for example, have allowed the wealthy to travel extensively to all parts of the world. The mass production and distribution of goods from automobiles to clothing has resulted in the disappearance of many upper-class status markers.

There are, then, aspects of tradition and change in the contemporary upper class. The upper class still retains its basic identity as a small, privileged segment of society.

THEORIES OF COMMUNITY COMPOSITION AND CHANGE

The analysis of land-use change has been a focus for a variety of disciplines in recent years. The need for understanding trends in land use—why they begin and why they do or do not continue—has been a primary requisite of the planning profession, whose members seek to guide the comprehensive development of land. In discussing the importance of understanding the determinants of land use, a renowned urban planner said: "If planning the urban community is to be dealt with intelligently, more than its physical structure must be taken into account. The forces that make, shape, and change the physical structure must be well understood."[14] The search for these "forces" that are responsible for land-use change has been the work of scholars from many fields.

Though the effort has been interdisciplinary in the sense that planners and social scientists have together been involved in it, it has not been coordinated. The members of the various disciplines have worked independently, for the most part, and have drawn basically upon the knowledge only from their own fields. The result has been a multitude of land-use theories that emphasize, if not entirely deal with, a single type of land-use determinant.

Economists are particularly noted for producing theories of this type. Their theories point to economic factors as the determinants of land use. Non-economic factors have traditionally been disregarded by these theorists. The consequence has been an "economic determinism" of land use.

Economic determinism maintains, in essence, that the forces of supply and demand are responsible for land-use patterns. The uses made of parcels of land are determined by the uses that will give the greatest economic return.

Economic determinism as a means of explaining land-use change became widely accepted in the first quarter of this century. This early popularity is understandable since the theory is based on a simple and direct relationship. For those wishing to go further, an attempt to measure in some precise fashion the levels of different land supply and demand could be made. The findings then could be graphically presented with the use of the economists' supply and demand curves. No wonder, with all these direct techniques, that explanations of land-use change through economic analysis became so popular.

The explanation of land-use determination offered by the economist was simple, but was it a complete explanation? This was the question that social scientists began to ask themselves.

Among the economically-oriented land-use theories that came to be reexamined in the light of this doubt was the famous theory of Burgess.[15] He asserted in 1925 that the land-use pattern of cities consists of a geometric pattern of concentric circles of different land uses surrounding the central business district. Since this central business district is always expanding through natural growth, the area immediately surrounding it is potentially of high value since it will eventually be demanded for commercial use. This area, labeled the "zone in transition," consists for the most part of speculative property holdings. Property owners here, seeking the greatest immediate profit, are little willing to make capital improvement expenditures. As a result, deteriorated structures are typical in this area. The various zones surrounding the "zone in transition" are residential areas, the more desirable being found at increasing distances from the "zone in transition." Burgess reasons that this will be the case since land values decrease as the distance from the central business district increases. Since the land in the more remote residential areas is worth less, owners are more willing to finance improvements there.

Recently, however, Burgess' analysis has been criticized. Debate has centered on whether Burgess' explanation of land-use patterns in terms of land values alone is entirely satisfactory. A typical criticism has been stated as follows: "While desirability of commercial property, or of industrial property, may be largely determined by economic considerations, the desirability of residential areas would seem to be a more complex phenomenon; quite general cultural factors would seem to affect residential desirability." This critic considers some of the physical characteristics of residential areas, such as detached homes and immaculate green lawns, and claims that these features "seem to reflect American cultural values rather than to reflect inexorable economic laws."[16] He concludes that social as well as economic conditions influence land-use patterns.

At least one proponent of this view, Walter Firey, compiled a land-use analysis to support this position. Firey attempted to show the influence of cultural factors on the pattern of land use in Boston.

Firey introduced his study by considering the concept of "economic rationalism" which has been the traditional explanation of land-use patterns. According to the rationalists, the most economically efficient arrangement of land uses will be the inevitable result of the free play of competitive forces. "The rationalists," Firey states, "have properly reasoned from their initial premises to the conclusion that every social system is forever struggling for a least costful location." But Firey questions the validity of the main premise "that the utility of the part coincides with the utility of the whole."[17] He feels that this is often not the case.

Though Firey attacks the utility principle as used by the rationalists, he has a more basic criticism of their position. This he states in the following manner: "They (the rationalists) have begun by regarding all social systems as purely economic units. They have then postulated that the only socially relevant quality of space is its costfulness as an economic good. From these two premises they have logically deducted that the city is a natural mechanism whose processes lead to a most efficient territorial layout of social activities."[18] Firey points out, however, that it is possible, indeed, not unusual "for man's use of land to deviate from a most economic arrangement." He concludes, therefore, that the economic explanation of land-use patterns offered by the rationalistists is incomplete.

In fairness to the rationalist position, Firey quotes such rationalists as Ratcliff and Haig as admitting the inadequacy of economic rationalism for completely explaining land-use patterns. Though these rationalist theorists agree that other than economic factors are involved, Firey criticizes them for making "no attempt to incorporate this empirical concession into their theoretical system. Their procedure has been the common one of granting a causative efficacy to nonrationalistic factors without in any way altering the rationalistic scheme itself." [19]

After introducing his report with a discussion of these broad concerns, Firey proceeded to study sections of Boston to determine how and to what extent social values have contributed to change in these places. Firey's findings were of two sorts. He found, first of all, that social values exert a direct causative influence on land use. The Boston Common, for example, has come to symbolize certain historic sentiments. The allegiance to these sentiments by the people of Boston keeps the land from being put to commercial uses. Another example of the role of values in shaping Boston's land-use scheme concerns the North End, Boston's Italian ghetto community. Whereas the preservation of the Common has been the result of a "fetishism" with the physical area itself, the North End has continued to survive because residence here enabled persons of Italian origin to become identified with the Italian community and its distinctive cultural values. As Firey states: "Those persons who most fully identify themselves with Italian patterns tend to remain in the North End, in spite of the deteriorated, congested conditions which prevail there." [20] On the basis of these and other examples, Firey concludes that "values are indeed self-sufficient ecological forces and that they have a very real causative influence upon land use." [21]

In addition to the discovery of a direct relationship between values and land-use patterns, Firey found that rationally functioning economic interests that appear to be behind particular land-use patterns stem indirectly from larger cultural systems. These interests, he maintains, are not self-given ends in themselves. To view them as such is to consider "social systems as passive, compliant and disparate adapters." [22] Firey is saying, in essence, that the economic productivity of individual parcels of land is influenced by general cultural conditions, such as consumption patterns. Such conditions make a parcel of land economically valuable at one time but can change to lessen its value at another time.

It is with these two sets of findings that Firey supports his view that social conditions play an important part in determining patterns of land use. Thus, social values, according to Firey, must be considered along with economic values to fully understand community change.

Even Firey's model, however, seems to lack the broad theoretic framework necessary for a complete understanding of community change. For one thing, he does not explicitly consider political factors as determinants of land use. Yet there is much evidence that political factors are very important determinants.

Real estate agents are especially aware of the land use implications of actions of planning commissions, zoning commissions, and other public bodies. An obvious effect of many of these actions is to significantly alter land values.

Political processes influence land use in a number of ways. By the use of zoning, the direct regulation of land use is achieved. Such decisions of public agencies as the location of public improvements like highways can significantly affect community change.

F. Stuart Chapin, Jr. is among those who have taken political as well as social and economic factors into account in the analysis of land use. Chapin sees the political, social, and economic spheres as consisting of three distinct groups of values. These he labels as profit-making values (the economic), public interest values (the political), and socially rooted values (the social). These various values lead to different types of actions which in turn produce particular land-use patterns. Chapin presents this process diagramatically.[23]

Chapin gives a hypothetical illustration of this process in operation. He considers a combine of builders motivated by profit-making values seeking to acquire at the outskirts of a city a sizable acreage of open land for development into a large-scale housing project including a regional shopping center. The first possible site on their list is ideal when viewed in economic terms, but not so from a political standpoint. Here they foresee difficulties in obtaining changes in zoning to permit the type of development they plan, and, also, they anticipate that prevailing public policies on extensions of sewer and water facilities will interfere with their plans. Thus, Site No. 1 is turned down.

CHAPIN'S REPRESENTATION OF THE
INTERRELATIONSHIPS AMONG LAND-USE DETERMINANTS

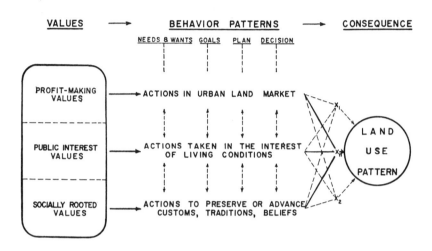

Though political barriers to their proposal are not expected in the case of Site No. 2, there are important social values associated with this land which could constrain them. A small estate community surrounds Site No. 2, of which several members of the combine of builders are respected residents. "These resident partners of the enterprise face social ostracism if they permit their profit-making values to prevail. Because of social symbols held by the developers themselves, this highly promising site is eliminated from consideration." [24] Site No. 3 is finally selected as a compromise between these various considerations.

The Chapin model has succeeded in taking social, economic, and political factors into account. But even this broad model fails to explain all instances of community change. Sometimes a land-use decision is made for other than social, economic, or political reasons. A few examples will be presented.

In 1963, Macy's Department Store decided to build a branch in New York City and began to buy up all the property on a prime five-acre site. With generous sums of money offered, all but one resident were willing to sell out. This person was Mary Sondek, an elderly mother of six, who lived in a two-story house on a 170 ft. by 50 ft. corner plot. Assuming that she was just "holding out" for a higher offer, Macy's went ahead with their plans to construct the store. But much to their dismay, they later found that Mrs. Sondek was unconcerned with the economics of the situation. Not even $200,000 could budge her. She simply wished to maintain her residence. [25]

Similarly, an old four-story building housing Hurley's Bar on the originally proposed site of the RCA Building in Manhattan was steadfastly held by its owner. Not even offers of $1,000,000 could encourage the owner to sell. [26]

There are many cases similar to the two examples presented here. These are certainly not as rare as generally thought. As one writer has stated: "Across the United States, virtually every city and suburb can point with pride — and sometimes alarm — at those who forced progress to step around them rather than let it walk over them." [27]

How can this "irrational" resistance to land-use change by the owners of these lands be explained? Certainly they are not motivated by economic considerations. Political factors generally have nothing to do with it. Finally, are these people acting in accordance with social values? It appears not. Indeed, their actions can often be viewed as being anti-social for they may very likely be preventing a new facility, commercial, entertainment, cultural, or otherwise, that the entire community desires.

If not for social, political, or economic reasons, what causes the holdout to act the way he does? The answer would seem to lie in the psychology of the individual. A psychological explanation might be as follows. Through various psychological processes, the properties of these individuals have come to have a unique and very important meaning to the owner. This feeling of attachment is so strong that he will strive to retain the property with fanatical perseverance in complete disregard of "practical" considerations.

A theoretic model of community change that fails to recognize the presence of "psychological" factors, therefore, is incomplete.

For, though it is probably the case that social, political, and economic factors are the most important determinants of land use, analysis that limits itself to these three sets of variables will prove faulty in certain situations.

THE PRESENT ANALYSIS

The present analysis of change on the North Shore will treat all four sets of variables. To make the scope of the present analysis any less than this would result in a misinterpretation of the facts. Social, psychological, political, and economic conditions have all played a part in causing the North Shore to change in the way it has.

Some people will be opposed to this treatment, maintaining that it acts to minimize the economic factors (which are admittedly often the most obvious considerations). This may very well be so. Yet these economic factors have largely been overemphasized in the past, almost to the point where other factors have been entirely disregarded. The present approach attempts to alter this, for it is not concerned with a single level of analysis, but rather with several.

Underlying this approach is the view that it is fairly standard to rely upon a solitary social science in formulating an interpretation of a social phenomenon. This, it is felt, has been unfortunate. The explanation that results is incomplete and, for this reason, distorting. Only a part of the picture is presented.

The present approach will utilize the knowledge of several social sciences. It will draw upon numerous theoretic orientations as it proceeds in an attempt to arrive at a complete picture of the change referred to as the "decline" or transition of the Gold Coast and a clear understanding of how this pattern began and why it can be expected to continue.

To reiterate, the decline of the Gold Coast, heretofore thought of in economic terms, will receive other treatments in this paper. It is hoped that viewing it from various perspectives will have the intended result of providing maximum insight and understanding. An attempt to synthesize these different interpretations will be made in the last chapter, although interrelationships will be noted throughout the book.

The decline of Long Island's Gold Coast has had far-reaching effects on life and thought on Long Island, and beyond. But, little literature dealing specifically and seriously with this subject has existed till now.

It is hoped that the multi-dimensional analysis performed in this study will be valuable in two respects: first, by providing a thorough understanding of the change that has taken place on Long Island's North Shore; and, secondly, by illustrating that the determinants of community change can be many in both number and variety. Before undertaking this analysis, however, the story of the Gold Coast will be told.

PART ONE

Gold Coast Development and Decline:
A Narrative

2

The Emergence of a Gold Coast

> *In order to gain and to hold the esteem of men it is not sufficient merely to possess wealth or power. The wealth or power must be put in evidence, for esteem is awarded only on evidence.*
>
> Thorstein Veblen

> *Give me the luxuries of life and I will willingly do without the necessities.*
>
> Frank Lloyd Wright

Before the break-up of the first large estates began in the 1920's, the luxurious estates of the North Shore existed unbroken. Residential subdivisions, schools, or public parks — none penetrated this community of extravagance.

These estates ranged in size from 20 to almost 2,000 carefully planned and thoroughly cared-for acres. They contained magnificent mansions with as many as 100 rooms and 30 baths.

The cost of these splendid monuments often exceeded $1 million and rose as high as $14 million, at a time when the dollar bought more — quite a bit more. These palatial residences had anything or everything from a golf course to an indoor race

track. With more than 600 lavish estates located on the North
Shore by 1920, the name Gold Coast was fitting.

Only at the turn of the century did the North Shore of Long
Island begin to resemble an estate area. And even at this late
date there were large tracts of vacant or farm land separating
many estates. Twenty years would pass (1920) until all these
open areas were substantially developed as estates. Yet before
1900, indeed well before that time, the North Shore and, more
generally, Long Island, was the locale of a few estates.

SOME EARLY ESTATES

There is a deed to an estate owned by Robert David Lion
Gardiner dated 1639. Mr. Gardiner also has a grant issued by
the King of England the same year. The land, deeded by the
Indians and granted by King Charles I (a contemporary of
Louis XIII), was developed as a manorial estate. It is the oldest
estate on Long Island and, possibly, in the United States.[1]

The original estate included Gardiner's Island, a 3,300-acre
island on the eastern tip of Long Island, and some 78,000 acres
on the mainland. This massive holding covered approximately
one-tenth of the Island.

A true manorial estate, the Gardiner holding was self-supporting. The main residence was located on Gardiner's Island; but
much of the land off the island was cultivated. More than 200
slaves worked the land. Because of its self-supporting nature,
made possible by its tremendous size, the Gardiner estate dif-
fered from the estates which emerged in the late 19th and early
20th centuries. These later estates never were conceived, much
less operated, with the idea of surviving by their own efforts.
Outside intervention was needed always.

Another difference between this very early estate and those
to follow later was size. The acreage of any one of the later
estates was only a fraction of the original Gardiner holding.
Although these later estate owners attempted to acquire as much
contiguous property as either their money or land availability

would permit, the limitations of one or the other usually made them unsuccessful in bringing together more than a few hundred acres.

The Gardiner estate, however, was similar to the later estates in some ways. Most notably, it was the scene of significant social events attended by those of prominence. Royalty was welcomed by the Gardiner family, on the same footing with high United States officeholders. Their visits were frequent. In fact, the Gardiners are said to have entertained George Washington when he was President and the late President Kennedy, in addition to many Presidents in between.

Although Gardiner was the first estate dweller, others did come relatively early in the history of Long Island. A few estates were created before the beginning of the estate movement of the late 19th century.

One of these was established in 1843 by the poet, William Cullen Bryant. Bryant's 40-acre estate, located in the Roslyn vicinity, was given the name "Cedar Mere." It is doubtful whether this estate was or could have been self-supporting because of its small size, even though dairy products and other essentials were produced there. Bryant, as "editor of the New York Evening Post and a poet of exalted reputation," certainly had a source of income independent of his land.[2] It is likely that a significant portion of this sum was used to maintain the estate.

THE NORTH SHORE BEFORE THE RAILROAD

Before the second half of the 19th century when the Port Washington and the Oyster Bay branches of the Long Island Rail Road came into existence, the area that was to become the Gold Coast was typical of rural America. There were farms and a few small villages and large tracts of undeveloped land. The North Shore was not a particularly good area for farming because the soil was stony and difficult to work and the terrain was very hilly. This general inadaptability of the North Shore to farming explains why the flatter, rock-free land of the South Shore was widely preferred as farmland and it early developed as such. Thus, some virgin woodlands were allowed to grow on the North Shore. These areas, with random patches of cleared farmland, proved especially attractive to estate site seekers.

Another characteristic of the North Shore before the Railroad was the prevalence of fishing villages. These hamlets existed near some of the well-protected harbors along the shoreline. Cold Spring Harbor, Oyster Bay, and Sea Cliff were such villages. Fishing provided a good livlihood for many families. A few were able to accumulate a degree of wealth through it. The Jones family of Cold Spring Harbor is a notable example. The members of this family developed a fishing industry while simultaneously involved in farming. Much of the profit then was invested in land on Long Island, and the Joneses eventually came to own large tracts.[3]

THE IMPACT OF THE RAILROAD

One North Shore branch of the Long Island Rail Road was completed to Glen Cove in 1871, and in 1889 it reached Oyster Bay, its present terminus. The other northern extension, to Port Washington, was completed in 1898. With these North Shore branches of the Long Island Rail Road in operation, the area underwent some change in character. The scenic hills, the quiet villages, the pleasant seashores were always potential tourist attractions. Transportation was now available to the tourist.

Oyster Bay, with a railroad station close to the shore, was especially attractive to visitors. Many people preferred Sea Cliff and Cold Spring Harbor, despite the distance of their stations from the shore, a condition which spawned another mode of transportation. A stage coach shuttle service was made available. Sea Cliff experimented for a time with a cable-car system.

A number of good-sized hotels began to appear in these new summer resort areas. In a short time, they became widely known and developed as popular and prosperous enterprises.

It is interesting to note that the Long Island Rail Road did more to popularize these resort areas than merely providing the means of transportation. Advertising promotions were employed in the last quarter of the 19th century to attract visitors to these areas. Numerous brochures containing photographs were widely distributed.

Beyond attempting to attract travelers to the North Shore's resort area, the railroad tried to entice homeseekers. Special commutation tickets were made available at extremely reasonable cost. But efforts of this sort were less than successful. There was still too much land available in the five boroughs of New York City, and, with the advent of the subway system in the early part of this century, parcels in Queens—"the land of the five-cent fare"—were especially sought out for home sites. The Long Island Rail Road simply could not compete. Moreover, before 1910 the Long Island commuter to Manhattan was unable to take the train all the way to his destination. For, in the absence of a tunnel to Manhattan, a short trip by ferry was necessary. Yet, these inconveniences did not discourage all homeseekers from considering the North Shore. A few, apparently accepting the inconvenience of commuting, did choose homesites here. But year-round residences on the North Shore for the average city worker were, for the most, uncommon.

THE WEALTHY ARRIVE

It was during the last quarter of the 19th century that the well-to-do began to look to the North Shore as a locale for estate settings. The first estates appeared in the area known then, as now, as Wheatley Hills. This area, though considered to be on the North Shore, is in actuality closer to the center of the island than to the northern coastline. Wheatley Hills was not very far from the railroad station in the small village of Westbury. That station became a terminus for many estate resident commuters as well as a receiving depot for commodities needed by the estate owners. The small town provided much of the labor required for adequate estate maintenance.

E.D. Morgan was the first to come to Wheatley Hills. He
established a 325-acre estate in the 1880's, and soon others
followed. Whitney and Phipps were among the pioneers, both
establishing their estates in the 1890's in the same area.[4]

Only a few estates were established in the Wheatley Hills area
before others began to develop in other North Shore locales.
Great Neck, Manhasset, and east as far as Cold Spring Harbor
each were boasting at least one good-sized estate before the
turn of the century.

These early estate settlers were drawn to the quiet rural area
of farms and woodland which was then the North Shore for
several reasons. One of the most important was the close
proximity to New York City. Owning a residence near the city
was an essential requirement for these millionaires in those
pre-jet plane days. For they were the big industrialists, bankers,
and financiers, and tied inexorably to Wall Street. The North
Shore, within easy reach of the city by rail, road, or boat, met
this basic criterion for the selection of a residence.

The North Shore had more to offer than convenience of
location. The land was rolling and wooded. This irregular
topography meant that each estate site in some way would be
unique. This was in contrast to the South Shore which, according to one early estate dweller, "is as flat as a pancake."
Picturesque the terrain was, but it was also desirable for other
reasons. Specifically it lended itself to the development of sporty
golf courses. The topography was also recognized as ideal for
the creation of an interesting system of bridle paths.

The North Shore was additionally thought to be a good area
for hunting. Indeed, since many wooded tracts were left undeveloped over the years, they became naturally stocked with abun-
dant game. This included rabbits, quail, foxes, and even deer.
Meanwhile, the shore area provided excellent duck hunting.
The North Shore as well as the South Shore of Long Island
traditionally have been well-known duck havens. One early
author said of Long Island that "the duck shooting surpasses

anything else on the Atlantic seaboard, owing to the fact that Long Island is the only land lying across the line of flight, and because its Northern bays, its Southern salt marshes and open water, close to myriad sweet-water ponds and feeding grounds, make the Island the only resting place for the birds on their long semi-annual trips." [5] But it is likely that more than for duck hunting, the shore area was attractive to estate seekers for another reason — the great attraction it offered to the yachts-men. The bays and backwaters, the safe harbors, and open outlets to the sound and ocean made the North Shore ideal for yachting. Prevailing southerly winds made Connecticut ports poor, for they offered little protection for boats. The same was true for many other coastal areas with land indentations.

Along the southerly edge of the North Shore near the center of the Island, another attractive natural feature is evident. This area was a part of the expansive Hempstead Plains. It was unlike the rest of the North Shore in two respects. First, the hills here rolled gently. Secondly, the consistency of the ground was such as to be remarkably suitable for using horses. Re-sponsible for this were the surface layers, including one of coarse sand and gravel at the bottom and a tough, springy sod at the top that produced a surface that was firm but not too hard. It is no wonder that the persons who established their estates in this area devoted a substantial part of their manor life to activities involving horses.

In addition to the advantages of topography, the climate of the North Shore was considered desirable. As a perhaps some-what prejudiced writer stated in an early Long Island Almanac: "The reasons why such extraordinary numbers of Long Islanders retain perfect health and unusual mental and physical ability, is in part due to the very even temperature averages, holding year after year at close to the same for each month in the year, with slight fluctuations in above or below the average in one month, brought back to the average in the following months." [6]

It is very likely that, apart from its implications for good health, this type of climate was vastly appealing to estate

people. It was important for these people to be able to predict
general climatic tendencies. For they usually endeavored to plan
at the beginning of the year where they would be at various
times throughout the year. Certainly, if they were scheduled to
spend "the little season" — the debutant season — in June on
Long Island they wished to have a general idea of what they
could expect in the way of weather at that time. Because the
climatic pattern remains relatively constant on Long Island each
year, this never presented a problem.

While on the subject, it might also be mentioned that Long
Island was considered to be relatively free from disastrous winds
and floods.[7] The supposed absence of these devastating conditions made the area a good place to invest large sums of
money on formal gardens and other precious appointments to
be found on most estates.

It was for these several reasons that many of those seeking
to develop estates chose the North Shore. Why, one might ask,
did the wealthy want estates at all? Some of the deeper motivations which were responsible will be touched upon in a later
chapter that explores the psychology of estate ownership. For
the time being it will suffice to reproduce some excerpts from
popular literature contemporary to the estate movement which
indicate some superficial reasons why estates were sought.

One article (written in 1900) is entitled "Country Homes on
Long Island — Where Weary Men Find Rest." This reported
on some of the millionaires who built estates on Long Island.
Through descriptions of their general goals in estate living, it
is concluded that there is a genuine pleasure derived from the
freedoms and broad possibilities of estate living. When speaking
of the Pratt brothers, founders of a number of contiguous
estates in Glen Cove, for example, it is noted that "when
tired of sport, they may turn farmers, though the farming here
is merely incidental and has for its main object the suppression
of weeds and the beautifying of fields."[8]

Another article of the period carries the title, "How a Businessman Became a Skillful Country Gentleman." It begins in
the following manner: "After a period of life spent in the city

in the all-compelling struggle for success, there comes to many a businessman who has finally 'arrived,' a lónging to get out into the open, away from the 'shut in' feeling of the town, where he can reassure himself that the blue sky domes above him in vast, unbroken reaches, instead of being a mere patchwork of ether glimpsed between grimy sky-scrapers."[9]

As the estate movement progressed, many articles of this type appeared in the popular periodicals of the day. Though a small part of this literature intimated that transforming a portion of one's wealth into a lavish, country residence was often done for social as well as personal reasons, most of the articles overlooked this possibility entirely. It remained for such social scientists as Thorstein Veblen, the American sociologist-economist, to clearly point to the preoccupation of people with upward social mobility as a possible motivating factor in causing them to display their wealth.[10]

Prior to being diverted to the broader question of estate seeking in general, the apparent reasons for the first North Shore estate settlers deciding upon this area for their estates had been considered. Obviously, the coming of these early estate dwellers has to be considered separately from those who came after them. For, when the later estate seekers came to the North Shore, they came to something more than farmland, woodland, and shore. With some estates already established here, the character of the area had undergone change. A Long Island Rail Road booklet of 1904 records this change. In the following two sentences quoted from this booklet which describes the North Shore, it should be noted that the first sentence could have been originally written several years earlier, but the second could have been added only around 1904: "Its characteristics are wooded hills, deep valleys with little villages nestled at the bottom of them, bold and precipitous bluffs fronting on the blue waters of the sound, and white beaches which form a charming contrast to the colors in the woodlands and the waters beyond. With picturesque indentations of bays and inlets, the North Shore has become the home of yacht clubs and country homes, many of them palatial."[11]

THE GOLD COAST EMERGES

It is apparent that the very existence of a few estates on the North Shore by the turn of the century added significantly to the attractiveness of the area for later estate seekers. The area was beginning to become known as a "Gold Coast." By 1906 — the year in which an extensive atlas showing property ownership and buildings on Long Island was published — many of the very large estates were in existence. These included the elaborate Guggenheim estate in Sands Point, the Mackay place in Roslyn, a few of the Pratt estates in Glen Cove, and a number of other large estates in Great Neck, Lake Success, Oyster Bay, Cold Spring Harbor, Syosset, and of course, Wheatley Hills.

Because the North Shore began to take on this new image, it was likely that a person seeking to establish an estate would naturally think of this locale. Certainly the emerging estate community there was widely known, for the purchase of a large estate site or the building of any estate of notable size was highly publicized. The following is a representative newspaper article: "The Harbor Hill mansion of Mrs. C.H. Mackay is fast nearing completion in structure and can be seen for many miles around. When finished it will surpass anything of its kind on the Island and will stand for centuries." [12]

Newspaper reporting of this type played a significant role in giving the North Shore a special magnetism for wealthy families seeking country residences. But this magnetism was, for some at least, based on something more than a vague sense of community and a desire to be among social and economic peers. Many persons had relatives who had settled on the North Shore. Members of the Pratt, Whitney, Vanderbilt, Roosevelt, and Phipps families followed the lead of relatives in coming to the North Shore. Close friends located there were also an attraction. Perhaps this explains why a number of Theodore Roosevelt's more affluent roughriders, like Joseph Stevens of Syosset, later came to live on the North Shore near the home of their former commander and close friend. Other individuals, meanwhile, were drawn by business associates who had settled here. It is not difficult to conceive that wealthy men for whom business played such an important role would consider the maintenance of important business ties in their search for an estate site. There are numerous examples of close business associates establishing estates in close proximity to each other. Officers of Standard Oil Company of New Jersey and J.P. Morgan and Co. were particularly noted for this practice.

There was, then, a sense of social, family, or business obligation that brought many of the later comers to the North Shore. Though it is conceivable that some would have come, and no doubt many did, aside from such considerations, their possible influence on many should not be overlooked.

The natural features of the North Shore that influenced the first estate settlers to come undoubtedly entered into the decision of later arrivals. In fact, these features were more evident to these later waves. The sites of the existing estates had been chosen and developed with such care as to enhance the beauty of the rolling hills and the other pleasing characteristics of the terrain. The ideal natural harbors for anchoring yachts now were in use.

By the turn of the century, many pleasure clubs had been organized. There was a club for every man: the yachtsman, the golfer, the horseman and the fox hunter. For the yacht owner, membership was possible in the regional New York Yacht Club or the North Shore-based Sewanhaka-Corinthian Yacht Club. The Meadow Brook Club came into existence in the 1880's and introduced fox hunting in the last half of that decade. Other clubs, such as the Nassau Country Club in Glen Cove, founded in 1892, were also established. As many facilities were added to each of these, they eventually came to collectively offer a great deal of varied recreational activities to the North Shore estate residents.

Before long, many widely-touted events were being held on the North Shore. These ranged from relatively small charity affairs sponsored by estate owners to international tournaments. Typical of one of the more celebrated benefits was a fair given by the Clarence Mackays of Roslyn on September 24, 1904. [13]

A number of estate dwellers and local villagers participated in this fete. Many unusual and costly souvenirs were given, including hand-worked leather goods. The day's proceeds went to the Nassau Hospital.

An early tournament-type event that brought much acclaim to the North Shore was the Vanderbilt Cup Race, an international automobile race. This annual contest, first held in 1904, brought worldwide renown to the "Gold Coast." It has been designated as the "most fully attended event in American Sports History up to that time." [14]

As a result of these highly publicized and prestigious happenings in an area that had already given rise to several notable estates, the North Shore of central Long Island began to be known as a "Gold Coast." This newly acquired title (reportedly introduced by the newspapers), in addition to the new swank clubs and other extraordinary aspects of the area which the title connoted, made the North Shore a very attractive place for an estate.

THE ESTATE MOVEMENT GAINS FORCE

Although this Gold Coast had its beginning around the turn of the century, more estates were established on the North Shore during the first two decades of the 20th century than in any other comparable period. The years between 1905 and 1915 were especially active.

By 1905 approximately 170 estates were located here. Most of these spread over 50 acres, and about 45 covered more than 100 acres. The pattern of development at this time continued to be based in part on business, family and social connections. Similarly, other environmental influences continued to be a factor. As time passed, the identification of the area as an estate community became stronger and stronger, the image being strengthened each time a millionaire moved in and developed an estate.

With the estate movement actively underway, the reputation

of the area for being a Gold Coast was beyond question. When one thought of the North Shore he visualized an "upper-upper" class, a playground for the rich, a place where multi-million dollar residences were common. This image with the prestige attached to it was more responsible than anything else for spurring the unprecedented estate development which took place in the first two decades of the century.

It is important that during this period significant improvements were made in transportation. The automobile, first of all, was developed and made available during the first years of the century. Roads were created or improved on Long Island at this time to form an elementary highway system. A few main access roads to Long Island from the city were built during this period. One of these was the "modern" Vanderbilt Motor Parkway. Although the building of this road which began in 1908 was planned for the purpose of using it for racing, the toll-paying motorist was allowed to travel on it.

As travel by road improved, railroad transportation also was modernized. It was in 1910 that commuting by rail to Manhattan was greatly eased. In this year the first Long Island Rail Road train passed through the East River tunnel and entered Manhattan. The need for the commuter to ferry across the East River thus was obviated.

These transportation improvements had some bearing on the further development of the Gold Coast during this period. Although many of the early estaters were extremely wealthy and almost semi-retired from their business life, this was not typical of estate-seekers of the later period. Whereas the early estate dwellers made periodic trips to the city, many who followed were compelled to travel there frequently.

There is much reason for doubting whether estates would have been built so rapidly in this period were it not for the new strides made in transportation. The car, the roads, and faster, more direct railroad service were therefore important factors. It might be mentioned as a point of interest that the Long Island Rail Road timetables of 1910 show almost no difference in travel time from that of today between North Shore stations and New York City!

Before the end of 1920, there were estates to be found in every part of the North Shore. The whole area had been transformed into one huge estate chain. Little acreage remained that was not a part of some estate. The Gold Coast of Long Island had become fully established.

Residences for the Rich

> *Their house was even more elaborate than I ex-*
> *pected, a cheerful red-and-white Georgian Colonial*
> *mansion, overlooking the bay. The lawn started at*
> *the beach and ran toward the front door for a*
> *quarter of a mile, jumping over sun-dials and brick*
> *walks and burning gardens—finally when it reached*
> *the house drifting up the side in bright vines as*
> *though from the momentum of its run.*
>
> from *The Great Gatsby*
> F. Scott Fitzgerald

The estate movement on Long Island, when the North Shore from Great Neck to Northport gained the name of "Gold Coast," occupied the first 20 years of the century. These were the years when the nation eagerly observed the North Shore glitter through all media. Americans were fascinated by the many multi-million-dollar residences being built and awe-struck as rolling, rural hills were transformed in ever-increasing numbers into well-manicured, palatial playgrounds.

Though the 1920's brought even more attention to the North Shore because of the gala parties given on Long Island by high

society, estate construction had all but ceased by this time.
Some estate land was quietly being sold, sounding the beginning
of the end for the Gold Coast.

It is interesting to pause before looking at the changes wrought
by the post-1920 era and examine the massive estate construction
at the height of the estate era. In all, more than 600 estates
were completed on the North Shore by 1920. Most of these
were more than 50 acres in size and at least 150 estates were
more than 100 acres. Let us observe how the multi-millionaire
who became interested in living on the North Shore at this time
went about selecting a site for an estate, having it developed
and, finally, operating the estate.

THE SELECTION OF SITES

There were a number of considerations involved in selecting
the land that would be developed into an estate. The prospective owner had to initially decide in what section of the North
Shore he wished to locate. In the early days without autos and
with a crude road system, this was an important factor. An
avid yachting enthusiast had to think of the hardship of having
an estate in an inland area such as Old Westbury. The trip
from home to yacht in these early days might take a few hours.
And, since the roads were far from smooth by today's standards, this was not a relaxing journey. Similarly, if it was necessary to make frequent trips into the city, to choose a site some
great distance from a railroad station, say on Centre Island,
would be a foolish move.

The advantages and disadvantages of living in various sections
of the North Shore were carefully weighed by the site seeker.
Generally, the yachting enthusiasts sought to be near a good
harbor, the water lovers chose a site with frontage on the
sound, and those wanting to participate in activities involving
the use of horses were attracted to the Wheatley Hills vicinity
where the core of the "horsey set" as well as the famed Meadow Brook Club were situated. Those who followed friends, rela-

tives, or business associates to the North Shore usually searched for a tract of land near their estates. A good example of a section of the North Shore which developed in this way is a small peninsula in the Oyster Bay vicinity (presently known as Cove Neck). The Theodore Roosevelt estate initially occupied a part of this land. Before long, other Roosevelt estates were developed in the area. This pattern continued to such an extent that the whole peninsula came to be known as "Roosevelt Country."

It should be pointed out that while the various sections of the North Shore were relatively isolated from one another, they did not remain so after the beginning of the twentieth century. Responsible for this change was the automobile. This new means of transportation made it possible to travel from one part of the North Shore to a distant part without great difficulty. Thus, the features and facilities of the varied sections of the North Shore could be enjoyed by all. Social interaction with friends, relatives, and business acquaintances became more prevalent because the distances between estates were no longer barriers. The question of where to locate on the North Shore became less important with the coming of the automobile.

In addition to the question of location, the site had to meet the buyer's personal criteria. Often, these requirements were entirely aesthetic. A series of small hills and sizable acreage of woodland were enough to satisfy the desire for beauty in most. Occasionally, a site containing at least one very large hill was sought. The idea here was to have the main residence built on this high point. This would insure a splendid view of the surrounding area. Other topographical preferences included terrains suitable for a golf course, a race track, a hunting preserve, or a small farm.

There were certain tracts of land that satisfied these requirements but were nevertheless considered undesirable. These were tracts that were near densely populated areas, or very close to railroad stations or other facilities used by the public at large. Leon Rushmore, a former owner of a large farm on the North Shore, told the author that he was never even approached to sell his land because of its close proximity to a railroad station.

After a site was decided upon the next step was to gain title to it. It is interesting to note that sites were considered with little thought given to whether they were actually "available." The procedure generally was to choose the desired site and then approach the owner or owners.

There was usually no difficulty whatsoever in securing the desired land. Farmers were especially eager to sell their holdings, for farming had become increasingly less profitable on the North Shore over the years. The stony earth was always difficult to cultivate. At the close of the 19th century, competition from other areas began to stiffen because the new national network of railroad lines made it possible to transport produce over great distances. Increased land taxes on the North Shore also made farming less lucrative.

The agents of the wealthy were therefore welcomed by the farmers. With reasonable sums offered for the property (and it was usually not necessary for the shrewd agents to offer more), a quick settlement was generally reached. The cost per acre was commonly in the $100-$150 range.

Though estate sites usually consisted of one or several farms or stretches of wood land, they sometimes contained other types of property. J. E. Aldred and W. D. Guthrie, for example, purchased in 1915 adjoining waterfront sites in Lattingtown (a combined acreage of 400) that contained sixty homes. The two wealthy men bought out each of the small home owners and demolished all of their buildings.[1]

ESTATE DESIGN AND CONSTRUCTION

After selecting and acquiring the site, an architectural firm specializing in estates was employed to develop a layout for the entire estate and to design the structures it would contain. The wealthy person would first confer with a representative of the firm and relate to him what kind of a theme he would like the plans to reflect. Also, the facilities he wanted on the estate were specified. Finally, the amount of money he was willing to spend in building the estate was stated. This last item was of little concern to most. Just getting what they wanted in an estate was their goal, without regard to cost. Thus, the decision of the size of the main residence depended more on the expected number of guests rather than the projected cost. Or, the decision to have an indoor tennis court depended on the owner's fondness for the game with little thought given to the additional quarter-of-a-million-dollar expenditure this would entail.

After obtaining the needed information from the client, the firm would blueprint the plans after due consultation with the landscape architects and regular building architects. The landscape architect had the most important task. It was his function to develop an overall scheme for the estate. His' first job in doing this was to order surveys of the site so that he could carefully study the topography. He then devised the plan. The key components of the plan were the locations of the main house, the other structures, and the connecting roads. According to Mr. Innocenti, a landscape architect who designed many early estates, "to fit the estate to the land was the essential goal." A contemporary article in a professional journal discussed some of the more specific problems that the landscape architect had to solve:

> The situation of the house in relation to the view, the exposure, the prevailing winds, the surrounding foilage, and other buildings; the situation of the garden in relation to the house, the exposure, the view and the trees; the scale and dimensions of the house in relation to the large planting; the extent to which the straight lines of an enclosure or of some subordinate architectural feature are desirable either to define the view, or partially to shut it out; the careful distribution of open and planted spaces in the immediate vicinity of the house; the use of proper planting, sometimes to complete and enhance certain native landscape effects, or sometimes to add a spectacular and dramatic quality to certain particular points of view; the lay of the approaches for the purposes both of convenient access and of the best effect; and the running

of the roads in relation to the grades of the land and
the making of entertaining vistas — the complete satisfaction of all these requirements or of half of them, is not
a business which an amateur, even in a petticoat, is qualified to supply; and the requirements of this kind, although less complicated and numerous, exist in the cases
of comparatively small estates as well as in those of
larger size. [2]

The architect presented the plan of the estate to the client
after it was completed. Often, it had to be reworked to satisfy
the client completely.

The task of the building architect, though less complicated
than that of the landscape architect, was also important. The
client stated a general design preference for the buildings as
well as the desired size. With this information, the architect
formulated building plans. These plans usually were subjected
to only minor modifications. It is not surprising that the clients
found little fault with the plans. For when good architects
(many with international reputations) are paid good fees (often
exceeding $100,000), the plans are bound to be good.

With the plans completed, a general contractor was engaged
to build the estate. Sub-contractors were then selected through
competitive bidding. Several hundred workers were required to
build a large estate, including many skilled men such as elec-
tricians and masons. For a really large estate, a big New York
City firm was often chosen as builder, since such a firm would
have the heavy equipment that was needed.

An estate took from one to several years to complete, with
an average being about two years. The estate might cost upwards of a million dollars. In the case of at least 100 estates,
this amount was spent several times over before the construction
was completed. The Tiffany estate in Laurel Hollow reputedly
cost thirteen million dollars. Both the cost and duration of construction were not determined by the size of the estate but
rather by the detail, artistry, and overall craftsmanship specified
by the plans. A gold leaf ceiling as found in the dining room
of the Woolworth mansion in Glen Cove or a marble Roman

styled outdoor bath complete with full-sized pillars built on the Guthrie estate in Lattingtown are two examples of estate details that added to the time and cost of construction.

THE ESTATES COMPARED

In comparing the 600 estates that were completed by 1920, some common characteristics become evident. All estates, first of all, included one large residence, and this was located in approximately the same place on all estates. It was usually placed in the center of the property if the estate was inland, or placed close to the shore if the property fronted on the water. The extended setback of the dwelling from the public roadway served two purposes. First, it allowed for an impressively long driveway to be built from the estate entrance to the main dwelling. On an estate of 500 acres or so, this driveway could stretch a mile in length. Second, the setback minimized the possibility of unwanted contact with outsiders. There is substantial evidence that the owners were highly preoccupied with keeping their estates exclusive. Armed guards might be employed to ward off trespassers. These trespassers were infrequently vandals, but, rather, local village people attempting to bathe on a stretch of private beach or picnic in a wooded area on the property.

Estates were also similar in that the other structures were centrally located around the main residence. Having all facilities in one section of an estate was considered the most convenient arrangement. Among the various buildings that were commonly included on the estates were servants' cottages, guest houses, greenhouses, and garages.

Although there were many features which were common to most estates, there were also vast differences among them. Most obvious here was the size of the estate. Estates were as small as twenty acres or were nearly as large as two thousand acres. It seems a general rule that the earlier an estate was established, the larger it was. Undoubtedly, this was so because of a decrease in the availability of land over the years. Yet there were exceptions to this rule. The largest estate was that of Marshall Field, established in the 1920's.

Estates also varied in architectural design. Among the more popular themes were Georgian, Gothic, Victorian, Roman, English Tudor, French Chateau, and Spanish. Sometimes, well thought-out combinations of these were adopted. The main house of the Coe estate in Upper Brookville utilized such a combination. A contemporary magazine article provides the following description of its interior:

> A feature of interest is the variation of styles in the interior. In this it partakes of the spirit of historic English country houses which have been built gradually over the space of centuries, beginning with old feudal times. The entrance hall is Norman, as if it were the remains of an old feudal keep; the bulk of the house is Elizabethan, as if the place had been extended and made more habitable later; and the dressing rooms and den are eighteenth century, as if they had been added in later and more formal days. [3]

Another difference among estates was the number and nature of facilities they contained. While some estates included a golf course, others had an elaborate sequence of formal gardens and orchards, others an indoor tennis court, others a large grazing area for a herd of prize cattle, others a polo field, and so on. It was extremely rare for one estate to be so complete as to have all of these things. Indeed, some of these facilities were incompatible with each other, for example, a golf course and a hunting preserve.

THE LOGISTICS OF ESTATE OPERATION

The operation of an estate required rather complicated logistics. It was necessary to coordinate the activities of the chauffeurs, gardeners, house servants, horse trainers, dog trainers, and other specialized functionaries, along with a host of laborers. To coordinate all these employees was largely the job of the superintendent. He coordinated the various estate functions, directed employees in their various tasks, and reported directly to the owner.

A large work force was needed to undertake the many tasks which had to be performed. The cleaning of the residence alone utilized many workers. Over twenty domestics were employed on the Frederick Clark estate (Old Westbury). Cooks were also required, not only for the owners and guests but for the employees as well. Men with assorted skills were needed to plant and keep the gardens, gather wood (estates often had a dozen or more fireplaces, a few of which were kept constantly burning), to tend to the livestock, and to do a variety of other jobs. The Pratts had a small five-man police force to patrol the 2,000 acres of their estates. Three chauffeurs were often employed on an estate, one for the owner, another for his wife, and the third just "on hand" for the use of guests.

The overall number of employees varied widely among estates. This total depended not only on the size and complexity of an estate, but on the intensity of its use. The work force on an average estate of 100 acres numbered between twenty-five and fifty persons. The largest estates employed upwards of fifty people, and in a few cases this total rose above 100.

The procurement of the key employees was another concern of the owner. Ideally, the superintendent came from England where he had already received training in estate management. Professional gardeners were usually Scottish, though these might be English or Irish. The common laborers were often immigrant Poles or Italians. There were instances of Negroes also being employed in this capacity.

The selection of employees depended on more than their availability. Owner's prejudices both for and against certain ethnic groups were often more important. The Aldred estate in Lattingtown, modeled after an English feudal estate, would hire none but English labor. Some owners would not have a Negro work for them in any position on the estate. The basis for many employment policies was an image in the owner's mind of specific estate employees — the Scottish gardener, the English butler, etc. This image was further followed by the use of uniforms, formal or informal, for virtually every employee on the estate.

Several of the more specialized workers lived in cottages on the estate. The chauffeurs, who were constantly on call, typically resided in units over the garage. Rooms in a designated section of the house were set aside for house servants. The day laborers, who were often seasonal (working from March through October), lived in a nearby town. Trucks from the estate were sent each morning to pick up these people.

The salaries paid to most employees were very uniform among the estates. Salaries of the superintendents, however, varied quite a bit, generally fluctuating with the size of the estate and the responsibility involved in the job. On the very large estates, these people were paid exceedingly well. In addition to the regular pay of $100 to $200 per week, a few were given a Christmas gift of a new car each year. The standard daily wage for day laborers was between $3.00 and $5.00 from about 1920 right into the 1930's, with just a slight temporary rise in the late twenties. There was never a problem getting workers at these rates. Some estates were apparently very flexible in the number they would hire. An open invitation stood at these estates for any able bodied man who was willing to work. The Brewster estate in Muttontown was such a place. It was soon nicknamed by the village people "the old men's home," for the elderly, unoccupied men of the town could always count on employment there when they were·in need of money.

Community in Transition

I am not now
That which I have been.
from *Childe Harold*
Byron

The zenith of the Gold Coast was reached in the years around 1920. By this time more than 600 estates with magnificent mansions had been established on the North Shore. Their cost to build is estimated to have totaled more than $500,000,000.

In the decades that followed, most of these estates disappeared, their mansions demolished, their land developed. After forty-five years of physical fragmentation the North Shore has changed almost beyond recognition and most people agree the name "Gold Coast" no longer applies.

What type of physical change has occurred to the North Shore in the last five decades? How did each decade differ in the amount and kind of change it brought to the North Shore? The discussion will presently address itself to these questions.

49

THE 1920'S: EARLY SIGNS OF DECLINE

The decade of 1920-1930, contrary to the usual commentary about the free spending during the "roaring twenties," was marked by a decline in estate building on the North Shore. The estates which were established during this period generally fell below those that existed in both size and splendor. However, there was one notable exception to this generalization.

Marshall Field established his Lloyd Neck estate in 1922. This was considered to be the largest (1,750 acres) and "the most complete" estate on the North Shore. About the only facility it did not include was a golf course. It had a hunting preserve, a polo field, a labyrinth of greenhouses, stables, a boat basin, a seaplane landing and more than two miles of beach. The main residence was appropriately massive for a large estate and even the guest. house would be considered a mansion by North Shore standards.

Most of the estates established in this period, however, were relatively small. With few exceptions none exceeded 100 acres. This contrasted to the existing estates, many of which included several hundred acres. Besides the reduced acreage, the structures on the places established in the 1920's were commonly fewer and smaller. The main residence, with little exception, usually contained fewer than 30 rooms. Main residences on earlier estates commonly had around 50 rooms, and not too rarely the number was between 50 and 100.[1]

It should be pointed out that there was some building activity on existing estates during the twenties. Swimming pools, bathhouses, tennis courts, guest houses, and additions to existing structures were among the items constructed on several estates. Winston Guest in Wheatley Hills added structures to his estate in both 1923 and 1928. A large swimming pool, with walls and walkways, was built on the Schiff estate in Oyster Bay Cove in 1928 as well. In 1921, the main residence of the T. Ashley Sparks estate in Syosset was enlarged with a new wing.

Changes to the North Shore during the twenties included more than the creation of smaller estates and the further development of existing ones. For among the many estates that transferred ownership during this period, a few were sold to other than estate seekers. These purchasers did not have the intention of maintaining the properties as estates. They had other plans. A few of these people were builders of small homes. Others sought to acquire land for recreational facilities, such as for private clubs.

The Munsey estate in Manhasset was up for sale in 1927 after the owner's death. Estate owners in the area made serious efforts to find a buyer who would maintain the 600-acre tract as an estate, but they were unsuccessful. Part of the land was sold to a syndicate which subsequently built houses in the $13,000 to $18,000 price range. Another part, including some of the main structures, was purchased by Mrs. William K. Vanderbilt, owner of a North Shore estate. She bought it to build a golf course for her personal use.[2]

A year later, another Manhasset estate was on the market. This was the 52-acre Cummings place. It was bought by a realtor named Breuer who soon developed it with small houses. [3]

The William Walker estate, a 200-acre waterfront residence in Bayville, was sold in the early twenties. A sizable portion of it was bought by the Bayville-Oyster Bay Realty Corporation that immediately began to develop it into a residential community of small homes. Besides constructing homes on it, the company sold lots to people wishing to build themselves. An advertisement in the *Daily Review* of June 24, 1924 reveals that the standard size of lots offered was 50 feet by 150 feet.[4]

Another estate fronting on Long Island Sound disappeared about 1925. This was the highly celebrated Paul D. Cravath estate. This estate was taken over in its entirety by the newly formed Creek Club. A golf course was constructed on its 200 acres, while estate buildings were converted into club facilities.

In addition to the estates that were sold and put to non-estate uses in the twenties, some vacant, unimproved holdings that might have very nicely served as estate sites were developed in other ways during this period. Such was the fate of several tracts, a few of them adjoining estates, that were sold at a huge public auction held in the second half of the decade.

THE 1930'S: A TIME OF INACTIVITY

The physical state of the North Shore in 1930 remained substantially unchanged in the decade that followed. Contrary to the image of the "bleak thirties," this is not altogether reflected in the physical features of the North Shore during this period. Though it is true that a number of estates cut down on employment during this time, very few estates actually went out of existence. A few even were established during that period, while some of those existing were further developed. It is significant to note that the proportion of estate building relative to small home construction appears to have been greater in the thirties than in the twenties, though, in absolute terms, more estates were built in the earlier decade. Also, on the average, the layout of the 1920's estates was somewhat more elaborate.[5]

One of the estates that was founded in the thirties was the Henry Phipps place in Old Westbury. This was not a very large estate (under 20 acres) but it contained a number of impressive structures. Among these were a 31-room mansion, a swimming pool, and a bathhouse. In 1931, J.L. Luckenbach developed a small estate in Lattingtown with a main residence of 27 rooms and a large greenhouse. Evelyn Marshall Field in 1933 created an estate in Muttontown. The cost of the main residence alone was reportedly $290,000. When the 30-room dwelling was inspected by a county assessor a few years later, he wrote in his report that "this is a very fine modern house throughout." [6]

Among the estates to which additions were made in this decade was the Harold I. Pratt estate in Glen Cove. In 1930, an indoor tennis court was added to this estate, and in 1935 the main residence was completely remodeled. Alfred P. Sloan of Great Neck had a large brick garage and a guest house built on his estate in 1933. In the same year an indoor tennis court was erected on the Merle-Smith estate in Cove Neck. J.S. Morgan, son of J.P. Morgan, added to his estate in 1930 and again in 1933. The later additions included a stable, garage, and stone walls. In 1936, William K. Vanderbilt had a major extension built on the main residence of his Centerport estate, expanding it from 7 rooms to 24. These added rooms had some very expensive features. The bathroom, for example, contained a marble bathtub with solid gold fixtures.

The 1930's, therefore, were not devoid of building activity on the North Shore in the form of new estates or the improvement of existing ones. But there were signs in the latter part of the decade that this trend would not continue. For some estates were placed on the market and buyers simply would not be found. The extravagant residences were apparently being demanded neither for estates, nor for small home subdivisions, nor for any other purpose. Only at prices greatly below those initially asked could they be sold. Organizations were typically the buyers. The Otto Kahn estate, one of the largest on the North Shore, is a case in point. It was acquired at a fraction of its original cost by an association of New York City sanitation workers to be used as a weekend and summer retreat. It cost Kahn $4,000,000 to build 22 years earlier, while the selling price in 1939 was $100,000, a mere one fortieth of that original cost.[7]

Also, some estate owners in the thirties endeavored to simplify their places. They engaged landscape arthitects to draw up plans that would achieve this end and still preserve much of the flavor of the original estate.

THE 1940'S: THE WAR ENDS, THE SUBURBS BEGIN

Because of World War II which occupied the first half of this decade, the span must be treated in two separate parts. During the first five years of this period, little change took place on the North Shore. The few estates that were disposed of were generally put to some institutional use and remained intact. The Chrysler estate at Kings Point, for example, was sold to the United States Marine Commission in 1941 and was used as a training center during the war.[8] Another estate disposed of in these years was that of J.E. Aldred in Lattingtown. In 1942, this 117-acre estate went in its entirely to the religious order of St. Basil the Great.[9]

So little change actually took place during the war years, 1941-1945, that the area could still rightfully be called a "Gold Coast" and viewed as an unfragmented, untrampled estate area at the end of the five-year period. Indeed, it was looked upon in this way. In 1946, in a 10-page feature article, *Life* magazine stated that "while more ostentatious centers like Newport and Saratoga have passed their prime, the North Shore continues to flourish, providing for those within its select premises a pattern of life that is ordered, gracious, and, amid great luxury, basically simple."[10]

Although it was the 1950's that was destined to fragment the configuration of estates, this physical process began in the late forties. In the years preceding 1950 a number of estates disappeared. For the most part, residential subdivisions replaced them. The outstanding Tiffany estate was among those subdivided. This estate, located in Laurel Hollow and Oyster Bay Cove, featured many magnificent structures on 1,500 acres of woodland and waterfront. Its cost to Tiffany was reputedly $13,000,000.[11]

A number of popular magazines took note of this trend near the end of the decade. *Holiday*, in 1948, commented: "The North Shore is still swank, but time is making some changes in its structure."[12] A *Life* article in November of the same year disclosed that many of the estates were "going begging."[13] *American Magazine* featured a similar article a month earlier entitled "Bargains in Dream Houses."[14] This article reported on a survey that was taken of estates on the market. The findings were that, on the average, the selling price was 25 per cent of original cost and only ten per cent of replacement cost.

The demand for estates to be held as estates, especially large units, was very low. They were bought primarily to be subdivided into as many building lots as the zoning permitted. A few of the estates that were sold were put to some use that

allowed them to be kept intact. Such an estate was Vanderbilt's in Centerport which was converted to a County museum
in 1949 shortly after the death of the owner. This occurred
because of the provision in his will which created a trust for
this purpose.

THE 1950'S AND 1960'S: COMMUNITY IN TRANSITION

The trend involving the splintering and overall reduction of
the estate area which began in the late forties, continued in the
fifties, and has prevailed to the present. In this period of almost twenty years numerous estates have been sold and converted to non-estate uses. Some of these estates were among
the largest and most elegant on the North Shore.

A number of these estates were sold for housing projects.
Included in this category was the island estate of J.P. Morgan
in Glen Cove. In the early fifties, the 54-room main residence
of this 110-acre estate went to a Catholic religious order, while
the rest of the island was developed into a small suburban
community called Morgan Island Estates. The C.V. Whitney
estate in Old Westbury was up for sale in the late fifties. A
developer similarly purchased a part of this.

There is an important factor that has greatly influenced
what type of buyer, and even what kind of builder, purchases
an estate. This is zoning. Indeed, the purpose of zoning is to
control land use change. In the estate areas that are incorporated (i.e., self-governing areas known as villages) the zoning
is typically very stringent and precludes many types of land
use. The more common prohibitions are the use of land for
industry and business. Thus, during the last two decades there
were no conversions of estates in incorporated areas to business
or industrial uses. Some estate land in unincorporated areas,
however, was sold to and used by business or industrial enterprises. Byron K. Stevens, for example, sold about half of his
estate (118 acres) which lay in the unincorporated community
of Jericho to a manufacturing concern. Estate land in East
Norwich, a small unincorporated pocket bordered on all sides

by estate villages, has also been put to a non-residential use. A gas station and a road-side restaurant are among the business facilities constructed here recently.

In addition to directly influencing the type of development that has taken place on estate land, the zoning has controlled the minimum lot size needed for residential development. The minimum building lot required by law since the late 1950's is two acres in most incorporated estate areas and is as high as five acres in two villages. A builder subdividing an estate must conform to zoning laws. It is for this reason that estates in unincorporated areas are preferred by builders. Here, with the more relaxed town zoning, they are often able to divide an estate into one-third- or even one-quarter-acre building plots.

Because builders have been unwilling to pay very high prices for estates in incorporated areas (compared to the amounts they have offered for those in unincorporated areas), many estates in the fifties and sixties fell into hands of other than home builders. These buyers had plans for projects that could not be thwarted by zoning. Sometimes they sought to establish a golf course or a private school, or if the purchaser was a government body the plan was to put the property to some public use.

Several private golf clubs were established on estates that were sold in the two-decade period. The International Business Machine Corporation (I.B.M.) created a course for its employees on the 204-acre S.A. Guggenheim estate in Sands Point. On a part of the C.V. Whitney estate in Old Westbury, the Old Westbury Country Club was established. The Woodcrest Country Club in Muttontown took over the 150-acre J.A. Burden estate in 1960.

Examples of estates being made into schools are also numerous. The Woolworth estate in Glen Cove was converted to the Grace Downs Model and Air Career School in 1959. In the early sixties, a 280-acre tract of the C.V. Whitney estate was taken over by New York Institute of Technology. The Coe estate in Upper Brookville was recently made into an administrative center for the State University of New York.

COMPOSITE OF A CHANGED COMMUNITY

This thirty-foot high wrought iron front gate at Old Westbury Gardens once admitted only prominent guests; now it is open to the public. (photo courtesy of Old Westbury Gardens)

PRIVATE ELEGANCE

Below — Twenty-six room Norman mansion on Harry F. Guggenheim's estate, Falaise, *as seen from carriage-house archway.* Mr. *Guggenheim intends to give to* Nassau County *his 90-acre Sands Point estate, including its manor house and art treasures, for the use of future generations as a recreational and cultural center. (photo courtesy of Newsday, Inc.)*

Opposite — The upper gallery of the great hall in the manor house at Falaise, Harry F. Guggenheim's *estate. (photo courtesy of Newsday, Inc.)*

PUBLIC SPECTACLE

Top — This elaborately-appointed building on the one-time Centerport estate of William K. Vanderbilt houses the former owner's fish collection and is now part of a Suffolk County museum and park. A touch, which some might consider eccentric, is a mound of grass on the roof over the entrance — the first tee of Vanderbilt's six-hole golf course. (photo courtesy of Vanderbilt Museum)

Bottom — The West Porch is one of the 32 rooms of the mansion built in 1906 at Old Westbury Gardens, once the private estate of John S. Phipps and now on public display. (photo courtesy of Old Westbury Gardens)

Opposite top — Summer lawn-parties were once a common occurrence on this now still south lawn at Old Westbury Gardens. (photo courtesy of Old Westbury Gardens)

Opposite bottom — Italian gardens at Old Westbury Gardens are planted with so vast a variety of flowers that they bloom from May through October. (photo courtesy of Old Westbury Gardens)

RUIN AND DECAY

Top — No ancient ruin but a crumbling staircase on the original Gustavia A. Senff estate in Muttontown. The steps lead nowhere, precariously attached to a foundation that supported a now leveled mansion.

Bottom — The Senff mansion, demolished by a recent speculator-owner to lower the tax assessment on the 500-acre estate, was built in 1906 and served as a prime example of Gold Coast splendor.

Opposite top — A destroyed cottage and barn and an abandoned servants' building on the former Senff estate, soon to be cleared to become a Nassau County park.

Opposite bottom — A dry and littered Roman Fountain surrounded by pillars that reached 10 feet are among the remains of the once-elegant estate of William D. Guthrie in Lattingtown. The only surviving estate building, the stables, is now a dairy company.

SUBURBAN DEVELOPMENT

Below — East Island in 1950, 110-acres surrounded by water was the Glen Cove estate of J. P. Morgan. The 54-room mansion was built in 1910. (photo courtesy of Lockwood, Kessler and Bartlett, Inc. and Nassau County Planning Commission)

Opposite — East Island in 1962, was transformed into a subdivision called "Morgan Island Estates." The mansion became a convent for the Sisters of St. John the Baptist.

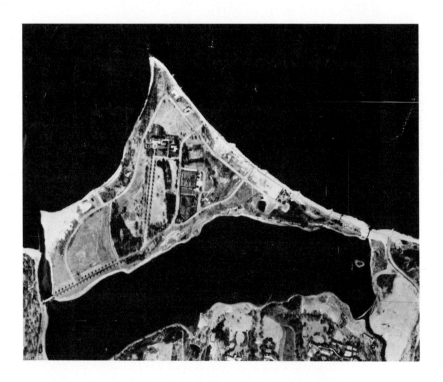

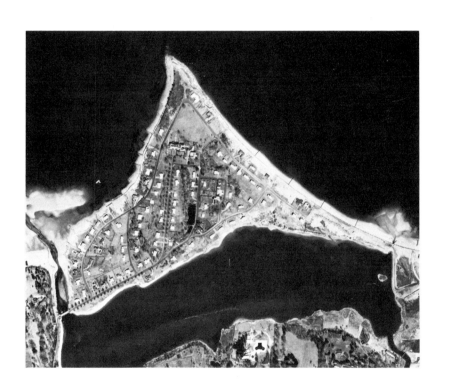

Above — *Suburbanites drive past the entrance to the former Otto Kahn estate on Jericho Turnpike in Woodbury. Built in 1917, the $4-million, 600-acre estate has been subdivided into a housing development, golf club, and military academy. The gatehouse that forms a part of the entrance now functions as a real estate office.*

Opposite top — *The large-lot subdivision of "Mill River Farms" in Upper Brookville distributes two acres of old estate land to each home.*

Opposite bottom — *The Long Island Expressway ("world's longest parking lot") winds through Old Westbury at the south edge of the original Gold Coast. By providing easy access to the area, the road has spurred extensive suburban development.*

HALLS OF LEARNING

Below — The main house of the former Marjorie M. Post estate in Brookville, now an administration building of C. W. Post College. It was used for classrooms in 1955, when the college was established. (photo courtesy of C. W. Post College)

Opposite top — Planting Fields, once the 409-acre Upper Brookville estate of William R. Coe, now is the State University of New York's International Center. (photo courtesy of The International Center)

Opposite bottom — Former stables of Cornelius Vanderbilt Whitney now are a part of New York Institute of Technology in Old Westbury. Retaining the Tudor exterior, the building has been completely converted to college use, housing classrooms, laboratories, workshops and studios, and is now known as Education Hall. (photo courtesy of New York Institute of Technology)

PLACES OF RECREATION

Below — The Woodcrest Country Club was formerly the Muttontown estate of James A. Burden. The Prince of Wales stayed in the 47-room mansion, now the clubhouse, when he visited the North Shore in 1924.

Opposite — The French chateau of Mrs. Roderick Tower now overlooks a ball court behind a public school. The grounds of the school had once been part of this Lattingtown estate.

A quiet walkway bordered by primrose at Old Westbury Gardens: For Long Island's Gold Coast, the path is uncertain. (photo courtesy of Old Westbury Gardens)

In Matinecock, Miss Stoddart's School (a private elementary school) has recently expanded onto the former Coffin estate. And, most recently, the F. A. Clark estate in Old Westbury, totaling almost 600 acres, was deeded to the University of the State of New York with its first classes commencing there in September, 1968.

Governments have taken over some estate lands. The 163-acre Daniel Guggenheim estate in Sands Point was made into a U.S. Navy special devices testing center. This estate is particularly interesting for its mansion which is actually a genuine European castle that was dismantled in Europe, transported to the United States, and reassembled in Sands Point when the estate was developed in the late nineteenth century. A small waterfront piece of estate property was purchased in 1960 for the village of Lattingtown's first public beach. The Town of Oyster Bay has also established a public beach on a part of the former Stehli estate. New York State has recently taken over the Marshall Field estate in Lloyd Neck. This 1,750-acre holding will soon become Caumsett State Park. A few public schools, as well as school district administrative offices, have been established on estate land on the North Shore over the last decade. Finally, public road building has consumed estate land. The widening of route 106, which runs through Muttontown, has used up over 20 acres of estate land in that village. Much estate property has also been condemned in Syosset and Oyster Bay Cove for the soon-to-be-developed extension of the Wantagh-Oyster Bay Expressway.

It is apparent from these examples that much change has occurred to the physical state of the North Shore over the last two decades. Many of the largest estates have been so completely developed that it is now difficult to imagine them in their former state. Though other places taken over by public or quasi-public agencies have not been so intensely developed, these have become the seedbed of much activity, bringing many users to the once exclusive properties.

There are still many estates on the North Shore today. In fact, the number is estimated to be above the total in 1920, as Table I reveals. But present estates are generally much smaller. Many consist merely of a few acres, a main residence, and a small greenhouse, garage, or cottage. Some contain no out-building whatsoever. These small estates should perhaps more accurately be labeled "estatelets."

TABLE I

NORTH SHORE ESTATES BY SIZE IN 1920 AND 1968

Size of Estate (in acres)	Number 1920	Number 1968
Under 100	442	625
100- 250	110	17
250- 500	30	6
500-1000	15	2
Over 1000	3	0
TOTAL	600	650

The number of estates has increased since 1920 because many large estates have been divided into two, three, four or more estates. This explains why the absolute number of estates is greater today than in 1920. But unlike 1920, estates no longer exist in a virtually unbroken sequence. Schools, small residences, wide public roads, and a host of other non-estate properties now exist in their midst.

It has been seen that the physical fragmentation of the Gold Coast originated in the twenties when the first great estates disappeared. After a lull in the early thirties, this pattern of change gathered momentum which has continued to the present.

The physical and social consequences this has had for the North Shore are many. The social consequences can be dis-covered by learning something of the life style of the estate dweller of today and contrasting this with the life style of his Gold Coast predecessors. Such a comparison will later be attempted.

The immediate focus, however, will be on the physical products of change. To learn of these, let us go to the North Shore as it exists today and observe its physical condition.

TOURING THE NORTH SHORE TODAY

A present-day tour of the North Shore is likely to leave a traveler impressed with the high quality and low quantity of development he will observe. But, if the visitor has made the trip in prior decades, his present experience will be disappointing.

Signs of change, of diminishing estate property and increasing non-estate development, will be apparent in practically all sections. Though, as viewed from the public roads, the remaining estates will show little fault, a closer look while on the premises will often produce a different conclusion. The buildings on many estates evidence a need for paint and repair. Stone stairways are often crumbling and foundations are cracking. Most of the glass of now unused greenhouses and garages is broken. The once carefully manicured grounds of many estates often show a need for grooming.

A tour of the North Shore might begin at the New York City-Nassau County boundary line. To travel east through the North Shore, one of three major roads may be chosen. Rather than take the Long Island Expressway or the Northern State Parkway which run along the southerly edge of the old Gold Coast, let us use the older North Hempstead Turnpike which penetrates the heart of the North Shore.

For six miles, driving toward the village of Brookville, this road appears largely as one continuous commercial strip. Much of this non-residential development has come about since the end of World War II.

Beginning at the New York City line, the village of Lake Success first appears on the right. This village was once entirely comprised of estates. Now it is fully developed with homes on small lots, save for a public and a private golf course and a few acres of vacant land.

Directly north at this point is the Great Neck peninsula. This peninsula was one of the first estate areas to disappear.

Much commercial and high density residential development (including several apartment houses) have come to exist here. A portion of land at the tip of the peninsula which forms the village of Kings Point is still very exclusive. Though few estates remain here, the zoning allows only residential development and requires that building lots be a minimum of one acre in size.

Moving further east on our chosen route we travel into the community of Manhasset. The non-residential development that borders North Hempstead Turnpike here is characterized by department stores and numerous churches. These facilities cater to the new suburban communities that have developed in the vicinity.

Located south just beyond the commercial development is the 575-acre John H. Whitney estate. This is the largest surviving estate on the North Shore and it is well-maintained. Directly south and east of this place is the estate village of North Hills. This 1,820-acre village is unique on the North Shore for its small amount of development. It has never had a subdivision in its forty-nine year history. Though most of its estates have disappeared, these have been preserved as private or public recreation areas. There are four private golf courses and a fine private tennis club in the village alone.

North of Manhasset is Sands Point peninsula which is made up of many former estate communities and villages. Though several private golf courses and country clubs have been established in this area, most of the estate land has been developed. Some estates still remain in the village of Sands Point, which covers the northern 2,700 acres of the peninsula. One of these estates is the still beautifully-kept Harry F. Guggenheim estate of ninety acres overlooking Manhasset Bay. Mr. Guggenheim recently announced that he will deed his estate to Nassau County with title to pass on his death.

Proceeding east along North Hempstead Turnpike we pass along the edges of two former estate villages. East Hills, to the south, no longer has a single estate. That portion of the village along the Turnpike now yields a string of commercial facilities, while its interior has produced small-lot residential developments.

To the north is Roslyn Harbor. This one-time estate village is now made up of a golf course and homes on one-acre lots.

At this point on the Turnpike it is easy to take a detour and travel north on Glen Cove Road. This will lead to the city of Glen Cove. Here one finds the southerly portion an older developed area. This area was developed in the early days of the Gold Coast as a residential area for those who worked but did not live on the surrounding estates. Directly east of this southerly portion of Glen Cove is the community of Locust Valley with a similar development history. Both of these areas now contain many deteriorating structures.

The traditional estate area occupying the northern half of Glen Cove has been largely developed according to restrictive residential zoning. Some of the land has been converted to industrial use. The cluster of stables ("the Pratt oval") used jointly by the Pratt brothers is now the site of warehousing activities. A complex of apartment houses occupies the nearby former estate land.

Of the half-dozen estates that still remain in Glen Cove the largest is that of the now elderly Mrs. Harold Pratt. Her 500-acre estate, built in 1905, contains many superb structures, including a main residence of forty-six rooms with fifteen baths and ten fireplaces. There is also a fine beach and a large modern bathhouse on the estate.

Another plush estate in Glen Cove is owned by the Russian Government which uses it as a retreat for its United Nations diplomats. This former Pratt estate of thirty-six acres contains a forty-nine-room mansion. Next to the estate is the newly constructed headquarters of the Glen Cove Y.M.C.A. Another adjoining piece of property contains another former Pratt mansion now used for the Glengariff Nursing Home. Across the street from the estate is the new Glen Cove High School.

To the east of northern Glen Cove is Lattingtown bordering on the Sound. Though there are some remaining estates in this large village, many of the original ones have been replaced by homes on two- to four-acre lots as required by the zoning. One of the former large estates is now a monastery, while another is a private golf club.

East of Lattingtown along the shore area is Bayville. This former estate village fell victim to rapid residential development with its lenient zoning. Some of the best beaches in Bayville are now part of public parks. Bayville ends where a peninsula incorporated as the village of Centre Island begins.

Centre Island is the most exclusive community on the North Shore today. The change that has taken place in this village over the last fifty years is negligible. This has amounted to only a handful of non-estate residences. No public or quasi-public facility has been established here. Estates and woodland still predominate.

If we were to pick up again on North Hempstead Turnpike directly south of this peninsula at East Norwich we would find that our detour has made us miss about five miles of the Turnpike running through the heart of the original Gold Coast. Many signs of change could be observed along this stretch, including golf clubs, large-lot subdivisions, and a college, all on estate land.

The college is C.W. Post College. A visit on the campus would reveal how fully the estate land the school took over has been developed with dormitories and college buildings.

The subdivisions in this and other parts of the North Shore could also be inspected. Most of the land they occupy is zoned for two-acre residential lots. Subdivisions now under construction feature standardized and "customized" homes selling for between $70,000 and $100,000. About twenty-five percent of the price is the cost of the land.

North and south of this five-mile length of the Turnpike from Brookville to East Norwich are numerous estate villages. A visit to all of them would reveal moderate to dramatic physical change. In addition to surviving estates, there are golf courses, colleges, and other institutions throughout these communities.

One of the communities in this area is Old Westbury. Here,

there are two major colleges, an existing golf course, a new one under construction, and numerous large-lot subdivisions among the remaining estates.

It is four miles to Suffolk County traveling east on North Hempstead Turnpike from East Norwich. Along the way, further evidence of change in the form of new non-estate construction can be observed. In a short trip south to Syosset, it is readily seen that substantial small-lot residential development has occurred here. Though a detour to the north will reveal surviving estates, including the 500-acre-plus residence of John Schiff, change is apparent in this area also. The more than 1,000 acres that comprised the famous Tiffany estate in Laurel Hollow are now covered with several hundred homes. The old estate structures are still to be found here, windowless and deteriorating.

Continuing along North Hempstead Turnpike into Suffolk County we come upon a string of nineteenth-century-styled shops which form the small business area of the old community of Cold Spring Harbor. Most of the small-lot subdivisions that can be found in this community are on former estates. Also occupying former estate land are a new public school and a home for the blind.

The land north of Cold Spring Harbor including the peninsula of Lloyd Neck comprises the still fashionable village of Lloyd Harbor with its few enduring estates. Its many estates which no longer exist have mostly been replaced by large-lot subdivisions. A religious retreat occupies one large estate. The largest estate which covered almost one-third of this 6,000-acre community is now the property of the New York State Park Commission which will soon develop it as a park.

Just beyond Cold Spring Harbor on the Turnpike we come into the business district of Huntington. With small office buildings and supermarkets among the new construction here, this several-block business area has become an active place. In the surrounding area can be found much new development consisting of homes on small lots.

Located to the north is the village of Huntington Bay. Few estates remain in this one-time estate village. At the entrance to the village can be found a now unused estate, originally called Ferguson's castle, with its abused buildings and overgrown grounds. Suffolk County owns the estate with its forty-room mansion after it seized it a few years ago for back taxes. Though its future is uncertain, a recent proposal is to sell it to a building firm that wants to convert it into a multi-family condominium.

The land bordering North Hempstead Turnpike between Huntington and Northport, the terminus of the original Gold Coast, has partly yielded to commercial development. Much of this strip, however, is still underdeveloped and retains its country character. The most obvious feature of the developed areas that border the road is the paved parking lot — parking lots for restaurants, professional offices, and stores.

A small number of estates exists north of this area in Centerport. Most of the former estate community has been developed with homes on large lots. A portion of its beach has been converted to a public park, while one of its most elegant estates, that of the late W.K. Vanderbilt, is now a museum-park administered by Suffolk County.

North of Centerport is a peninsula made up of Eatons Neck and the estate village of Asharoken. In order to arrive on this peninsula we must pass through Northport.

Many new homes on three-quarter-acre lots have been built in Asharoken, squeezing out most of its estates. Eatons Neck which sits at the end of the peninsula is entirely developed with homes, save for a large public beach.

As we passed through the Gold Coast on our brief tour, the reduction and fragmentation of the original estate area was evident everywhere. It must be concluded that the physical change on the North Shore over the last fifty years has been substantial.

5

Patterns of Living Past and Present

Feast, and your halls are crowded;
Fast, and the world goes by.

from *Solitude*
Ella Wheeler Wilcox

Only physical change on the North Shore over the last forty-five years has thus far been considered. No direct attention has been given to social change. But change in the living patterns and social life of estate dwellers has also been significant. This social transition is important to consider for it appears closely interrelated with the physical change already described.

The meaning of the phrase "decline of the Gold Coast" is based largely on physical change, for "Gold Coast" refers to a geographical area. But it implies some degree of social change as well. We have already seen that on physical grounds the phrase "decline of the Gold Coast" has much validity. Let us now see how its use might be applicable to other than the physical aspects of the North Shore.

In this chapter we shall seek to discover in what way and to what extent the life style of an estate dweller has changed. It will be made clear that at least a part of this change is rooted in the physical change which has been disclosed. Life on the Gold Coast around 1920 will first be considered. It appears that although the climax of Gold Coast life was reached just before the First World War, everything was still at its height in the few years that followed. At least this is the opinion of the more than 100 estate owners and superintendents interviewed for this book, several of whom lived on the North Shore as early as this period.

ESTATE LIFE CIRCA 1920

Before discussing what life was like for a North Shore estate dweller around this time, it is important to consider what portion of the year these early Gold Coast dwellers actually spent on Long Island. The owner of a North Shore estate commonly maintained a summer residence in Bar Harbor, Maine or Newport, Rhode Island ("a summer resort without a single summer hotel"[1]) and a New York City apartment for winter use. It was during the spring and early fall that the estate on the North Shore was occupied. In addition to these two periods, many winter weekends were passed on the estate.

Although less than one-quarter of the year was spent on the North Shore (and in some cases it was as low as one-twelfth), it seems that here was the base for most of the rich. This has been disclosed in current interviews with estate persons who lived through this period. Further evidence is that many estate people voted as residents of the North Shore.

With the North Shore as their base, these families migrated together throughout the year to other chosen locales. This produced close and extended social interaction among these people and created a strong self-identity as a unified social group.

Though instances of independent travel to places abroad were common, these were almost always undertaken in the quiet winter months when social obligations were relaxed. An important social event such as a party in honor of an international personality or member of royalty found almost 100 per cent membership participation.

The North Shore of this time was often described as "the playground for the rich." It will be seen shortly why this description was entirely accurate. First, let us see the work of the heads of estate households and how the trip from North Shore to New York City was made. Commuting was done in a variety of ways. Some did it in a chauffeured limosine. Others used the private coach cars of the railroad. The twenty-five or so millionaires who might occupy a private railroad car usually became very intimate with each other. One early estate owner interviewed who was a member of such a group recalled how he knew in detail the political dispositions of all his fellow travelers.

A number of men who owned places on or near the water regularly made the trip to the city by private boat. Sometimes one craft would be used to transport a few persons. *Dodger,* Harold I. Pratt's yacht, was used in this way. Each morning his brothers (owners of bordering estates) and a few nearby estate owners such as J.P. Morgan, Davison, and Aldred would board the boat. They returned in the late afternoon. This was no doubt a pleasant way to travel. The operation of the craft was left completely to a seven-man crew.

Marshall Field's waterfront estate was located further out on the Island, about 40 miles from Manhattan. Although he too commuted by boat for a time, he later came to use a seaplane for this purpose.

The social and recreational activities available to the estate people on the North Shore at this time were many. The estate people were avid publicity seekers judging from the complete coverage their activities received. The result was that knowledge of what the wealthy were collectively doing could be obtained by any person who could afford a daily newspaper and knew how to read. A current newspaper reporter remarked after considering the highly publicized affairs of the estate people that "although the feudal-like places may have been erected to keep the public out, little that happened in them was private." [2]

Among the standard recreational activities engaged in by estate people, those involving the use of horses were a predominant pastime for many. These sports included polo, fox hunting, racing, and horseback riding. Polo, as a competitive sport, was attractive to many. In order to play you did not have to be a good athlete, but merely the owner of a well-trained horse.

Other land sports were golf, tennis (three varieties of which were indoor, clay, and lawn), skeet shooting, and hunting. Yachting and fishing were popular water sports.

An estate resident might participate in all these recreational activities either on his own or as a member of a club. Private recreation facilities were common on many estates. Large swimming pools and tennis courts were practically standard features of estates. At least a dozen estates had indoor tennis courts which cost up to a half million dollars to build. The indoor tennis court on the Harold Pratt estate had a wing that housed a badminton court. A number of estates had full-size, eighteen-hole golf courses. W.K. Vanderbilt of Centerport had his golf course situated in a way that allowed him to tee off for the first hole from· a second-story balcony of his private clubhouse. Private polo fields and race tracks were common on the North Shore. One indoor race track was actually built. This was on the Old Westbury estate of H.P. Whitney who had the exterior of the low, sprawling building styled in English tudor to conform to the other estate structures.

The private clubs on the North Shore, meanwhile, offered additional facilities and made it possible for the estate owner to participate in sports with others. The Sewanhaka-Corinthian was designed for the yachtsman, the Creek for the golfer, the Piping Rock for the golfer as well as the horseman, and the Meadow Brook for the horseman, principally the fox hunter. Any or all of these and other clubs might be joined by the estate owner.

The Meadow Brook Club, "formed to support and hunt a

pack of fox hounds in the proper seasons and to promote other out-door sports," could be joined, if approved by the Board of Governors, by paying an initiation fee of $250. The maximum number of members was fixed at 200 and the yearly dues were $200. If a member for ten years, lifetime membership might be obtained by paying $2,500. There were 109 regular members of this club in 1924.[3] Each year the club sponsored the famous Meadow Brook Hunt. The participants in this event had the permission of the estate owners to ride across their properties. Also cooperating to make this event a success were the Nassau County police. They stopped traffic on the major North Shore roads like North Hempstead Turnpike while the hunting party crossed over in pursuit.

The Piping Rock Club, restricted to 700 regular male members, required new members to pay an initiation fee of $300 and, after June 20, 1921, to subscribe to $1,000 worth of club stock. Annual dues amounted to $250. In 1922, 675 members were listed in the club book.[4]

In addition to offering sports facilities, clubs served as places where members and guests engaged in social intercourse. These were informal meetings. The more formal gatherings were held on the private estates. These meetings took the form of one sort of celebration or another. Some of the more common affairs were given for engagements, weddings, and debuts. But, though these were regular in the sense that they were held frequently, they were often quite lavish. Expensive jewelry was given away as favors to the ladies. Alternating orchestras provided continuous music. Often, well-known personalities in the entertainment world were employed to perform. Enrico Caruso appeared at the party given by Otto Kahn for his daughter who made her debut in 1922. He sang two songs at a cost of $10,000 to Kahn.

Special parties were given in honor of internationally known figures when they visited the North Shore. When Charles Lindberg returned to America after his heroic flight in 1927 he was welcomed by the estate people at a dazzling party given by Clarence Mackay. Many parties were held in honor of the

Prince of Wales during his extended visit to the North Shore in 1924.

Though many members of royalty came to visit the North Shore, the Prince of Wales' stay was perhaps the most socially significant. Many published accounts of his visit exist. Using excerpts from one of these accounts, a description of this North Shore episode follows:

> As soon as the public health doctors cleared the *Berengaria* at quarantine the Prince stepped down a ladder to a tug and was then put aboard the beautiful *Black Watch,* owned by Robert Graves, millionaire wallpaper manufacturer. The yacht was to take him to Glen Cove and the rest of the trip to the Burden estate at Syosset was to be made by motorcar.

The Prince landed at the private pier of Herbert Pratt. This occurred to the disappointment of a large crowd who expected him to land at a public pier about a mile away. The 10-mile stretch of road from Glen Cove to Syosset was carefully cleared by police.

> While in the country the Prince of Wales occupied the house of James Abercrombie Burden at Syosset, within convenient distance of the Meadow Brook Club where the polo matches were played. Mr. and Mrs. Burden, who were in Europe, put their establishment — Colonial mansion, 140 acres of wooded hills, autos, stables, servants, horses, all at his disposal. Colonel H. Rogers Winthrop, President of the Piping Rock Club, was his host. [5]

The gala parties that were a regular feature of North Shore life at the time received great notoriety. These costly affairs provided the best in food, drink, and entertainment. Elaborate decorations were also featured. A newspaper description of the physical setting of one party in Huntington stated that "the decorations were novel to the extreme." [6]

Novelist F. Scott Fitzgerald lived on the North Shore in the mid-twenties and used the area as the setting for *The Great Gatsby*. Undoubtedly, the parties and personalities described by

Fitzgerald in his book were a composite of his own North Shore experiences. Thus, the party he describes is probably very typical of such events on the North Shore in this period.

In referring to North Shore estate owner Jay Gatsby, he relates that:

> On week-ends his Rolls-Royce became an omnibus, bearing parties to and from the city between nine in the morning and long past midnight, while his station wagon scampered like a brisk yellow bug to meet all trains. And on Mondays eight servants, including an extra gardener, toiled all day with mops and scrubbing-brushes and hammers and garden-shears, repairing the ravages of the night before.
>
> Every Friday five crates of oranges and lemons arrived from a fruiterer in New York — every Monday these same oranges and lemons left his back door in a pyramid of pulpless halves. There was a machine in the kitchen which could extract the juice of two hundred oranges in half an hour if a little button was pressed two hundred times by a butler's thumb.
>
> At least once a fortnight a crop of caterers came down with several hundred feet of canvas and enough colored lights to make a Christmas tree of Gatsby's enormous garden. On buffet tables, garnished with glistening hors d'oeuvre, spiced baked hams crowded against salads of harlequin designs and pastry pigs and turkeys bewitched to a dark gold. In the main hall a bar with a real brass rail was set up, and stocked with gins and liquors and with cordials so long forgotten that most of his female guests were too young to know one from another.
>
> By seven o'clock the orchestra has arrived, no thin five-piece affair, but a whole pitful of oboes and trombones and saxophones and viols and cornets and picolos, and low and high drums. The last swimmers have come in from the beach now and are dressing up-stairs; the cars from New York are parked five deep in the drive, and already the halls and salons and verandas are gaudy with primary colors, and hair shorn in strange new ways, and shawls beyond the dreams of Castile.... Once there they were introduced by somebody who knew Gatsby, and after that they conducted themselves according to

the rules of behavior associated with an amusement park. Sometimes they came and went without having met Gatsby at all, came for the party with a simplicity of heart that was its own ticket of admission.[7]

In addition to parties and the regular sports activities, there were numerous special events which took place on the North Shore. Such events included various tournaments, flower shows, horse shows, dog shows, and special charity affairs. One horse show sponsored yearly by the Huntington Bay Club drew over 200 entries from all over the northeastern seaboard.[8] These events occupied the time of many estate dwellers. Often, they were carefully planned and publicized well in advance.

ESTATE LIFE NOW

It is difficult to generalize about the living patterns of North Shore estate dwellers today. The present estate people on the North Shore, unlike those of the earlier period, do not share a common pattern of living. There are elderly estate owners who spend substantially all their time on their North Shore place. Mrs. H.I. Pratt of Glen Cove and Mrs. Bonney of Oyster Bay, before her death in 1967, typified such owners. There are still some owners, on the other hand, who follow in the old tradition of living on Long Island during certain periods of the year. But even this group is dissimilar in that the members do not have their off-North Shore residences in the same place. Some persons, therefore, spend time in Florida, others in Maine, and in various other areas.

In addition to these two types, one of which stays on Long Island all year long and the other seasonally migrating as in the old days, a third group of estate residents exists. These individuals occupy their places sporadically without any overall preconceived pattern. Members of this final category do a great deal of traveling and, these days, rely heavily on the jet plane. They sometimes have an apartment in Paris, Rome, and other world centers or a small villa on the Mediterranean or in the West Indies.

Thus, heterogeneity is found even before viewing the characteristics of North Shore living of estate dwellers. For there are gross differences in the amount of time actually spent on Long Island. This means, among other things, that large cliques of estate people who lived and seasonally migrated together, are no longer to be found. Even in those instances when these people are on the North Shore together they do not form a homogeneous group. Their attitudes and interests are strikingly diverse. Responsible for this in part is that these people are now of many different age groups. There are several very young estate owners, many middle-aged ones, and a surprisingly large number who are over eighty years old.

Also contributing to the disappearance of large coteries is the fact that fewer large estates remain on the North Shore. Where one large estate was there are now often a number of small homes. The estate village of Lattingtown, for example, was the site of 366 newly-constructed, non-estate residences in the 20-year period between 1946 and 1965. In the same period, new non-estate residential construction took place in the other estate communities. Bayville yielded 974 homes, Sands Point 489, Old Westbury 395, and Roslyn 221. One former estate village, East Hills, has been completely developed with more than 1,700 homes.[9]

These new homes are owned and occupied by persons whose income and status is typically much lower than that of estate people. It would be socially dangerous for the estate owners to associate with these new neighbors as closely as they were accustomed to doing with the old (estate) neighbors.

Besides the influx of a lower socio-economic class inhibiting the formation of big social sets, the very increase in North Shore population has also contributed to this. At the height of the estate era only about 600 upper-class families existed on the North Shore. Such a small number facilitated the creation of major interrelated social groups. Such closely knit social organization for the entire North Shore is now all but impossible with the tremendous increase in population. The increases in population for the estate villages shown in Table II are representative.

TABLE II

POPULATION OF SELECTED ESTATE VILLAGES		
Village	1930	1965
Sands Point	438	2,447
Mill Neck	516	956
Old Brookville	423	1,359
Matinecock	484	869
Lloyd Harbor	480	3,124 (1967 total)

source: United States Bureau of the Census

The disappearance of large social circles is just one aspect of the change in North Shore life. Much has also changed in the realm of society affairs. Social events have come to be sponsored by associations rather than by individuals. Not only has this meant less control over those who can attend, but that a great deal less money is spent on them.

A few estate owners continue to give their own parties. These affairs, however, do not compare in lavishness with those of bygone days. It is not unusual for estate people to hold these affairs off their estates, Clubhouses are often rented for the evening. Even when estates are used for parties, caterers are commonly called upon to provide the food, drink, and services. Estates are now inadequately staffed for owners to do this themselves. These parties are not only less extravagant, but they are far more informal. The guest lists are also much smaller.

Though live entertainment is still common at parties, this is now provided by a small band. This is a striking contrast to the full orchestra and internationally famous performers that were employed in the past.

Recreation activities have also changed on the North Shore. Polo has virtually vanished. The case of the Bostwich family of Old Westbury is typical. The elder Bostwich was said to be a renowned polo player and horseman. His two sons have reportedly taken up and have become very skillful at golf. This sport has become the modern-day polo for many estate people.

There is still an annual Meadow Brook hunt. But the event is not as it once was. Because the contigous arrangement of estates has been broken, the participants are confined to a relatively small area. The hunters are also significantly fewer in number.

It is noteworthy that none of the clubs that were around in the 1920's have gone out of existence. As a matter of fact, over a dozen new ones have been established since then. There is one club, The Glen Oaks Club, that is under construction at present on 247 acres of former estate property in Old Westbury. Most of these private clubs feature golf courses.

The old clubs have changed. The facilities of many have become reduced in number and quality. All these clubs have become less exclusive. Once they had long waiting lists. Now some search hard for members. Because of this, they are less discriminatory. Even initiation fees have been relaxed over the years so that more people could afford to join. Some clubs have become flexible in regard to dues and are allowing men under a certain age (e.g., thirty-five at the Piping Rock Club) to pay less than other members.

The new clubs are merely "country clubs." When this title is applied to the old clubs, its members take offense, for there are essentially no social barriers on who can join these newest establishments. They are usually set up for the golf enthusiast. Only standard clubhouse facilities are provided.

Individual private recreation facilities, formerly a common feature of the estates, are often found in unserviceable condition today. These have deteriorated through lack of maintenance and use. Some have been taken over by local groups. The indoor tennis court on the Mrs. Harold Pratt estate has been kept up in this way.

The new facilities currently being built on the North Shore are products of private and public organizations and not projects of private individuals. As a Long Island historian has stated: "Today instead of the indoor swimming pools and tennis courts and the tile-lined anchorages which such wealthy families provided for their guests, the tendency is to create recreation facilities for all to use, the money provided by some government or other—maybe state, or maybe county, town, or village." [10]

The evidence here presented clearly indicates that North Shore estate living has changed. It is therefore apparent that the decline of the Gold Coast is more than a physical phenomenon. It has unquestionably involved some measure of social change to the extent that the patterns of living and social organization of the estate dwellers today is different than it was formerly. Social pursuits, activities, and obligations have changed dramatically. Most strikingly, these are no longer uniform among the members of the estate community. This is to be expected since the very social structure of the community has changed. No longer is the North Shore the homogeneous community of millionaire upper-class individuals it once was. The conversion of a number of estates into residential subdivisions has brought a large number of less affluent, non-upper-class people into the area. Thus, just as the physical structure of the North Shore has become heterogeneous, so has its social structure become diversified. Symptomatic of this change has been the changes in the patterns of estate living.

As for a general descriptive statement to denote this overall change in Gold Coast living, various possibilities exist. That "High society on Long Island has tired blood" has been suggested by one source. [11] In that *Newsday*, Long Island's principal daily newspaper, no longer contains a society page, this statement receives support additional to that provided in this chapter.

PART TWO
The Decline:
An Interpretation

Introduction to Part II

The book to this point has attempted to describe the change, primarily physical but also social, that has been taking place on Long Island's North Shore. It may be concluded from the material presented that the North Shore which once existed as a Gold Coast has not survived as a Gold Coast. The difficult question remains to be answered: Why the decline?

For anything to remain in existence, whether it is a living organism, a social organization, or, as in the Gold Coast case, a special upper-class community, certain conditions must be present. The human being, for example, is dependent upon oxygen and food. Much in the same way, survival of the Gold Coast depended on certain conditions. These conditions will be the concern of the rest of this book. An attempt will be made to identify them and to evaluate them in terms of what impact their dissolution has had on the Gold Coast.

It is the central thesis of this book that certain political, social, psychological, and economic conditions were essential to the survival of Long Island's Gold Coast. With the gradual disappearance of these requirements, the Gold Coast increasingly became an anachronism and was doomed. It will be pointed out, however, that not all of these conditions have disappeared entirely. In particular, certain psychological factors seem still to be present. These conditions appear to motivate owners of estates to steadfastly hold on to their properties, even though their estates may have become increasingly less desirable from social and economic standpoints.

The continued presence of these and other conditions explains why the estate community has been fragmented and reduced, not totally dissolved.

Just as Part I identified the change that has taken place on the North Shore as a gradual process rather than a sudden phenomenon, it will now become clear that the conditions underlying this movement also have changed gradually. Because this process has been very gradual, the problem of analyzing it is complex.

Adding to this complexity is the interdependence of the political, social, and economic conditions to be examined. Although, as the chapter titles reveal, these various conditions are viewed essentially in isolation, attempts regularly will be made to show the nature and extent of interdependence. In the final chapter a systematic effort at interdisciplinary analysis will be made. This chapter will be concerned in its entirety with an assessment of the collective influence of all previously examined conditions on the decline of the Gold Coast.

The interdependence of two different conditions, the one social and the other economic, may be illustrated as follows. The attitudes of people in the labor market toward working on an estate heavily determine their availability for such work. Thus, attitudes (a social condition) can directly influence the supply of labor (an economic condition). If attitudes toward this type of work are becoming increasingly unfavorable, as later will be shown to be the case, the effect will be a decrease in the supply of laborers for estates. If the demand for this type of labor remains constant while the decrease is occurring in the supply, higher wages will have to be offered by estate owners to secure the needed help.

Part II is divided into four chapters. Each chapter deals extensively with one of the four groups of factors that have played a role in reducing and fragmenting the North Shore estate area. Though the evidence supporting the role played by some factors is greater than for others, all "apparent" contributing factors will be discussed so that the possibility of their influence will be recognized.

The first chapter of Part II considers political conditions. It is a generally accepted fact that political conditions are important determinants of physical (land-use) change and economic and social change, as well. Changing political conditions, therefore, can have far-reaching consequences. An attempt will be made to identify many of these conditions and explain how and to what extent they have contributed to the change that has occurred on the North Shore.

In another chapter economic factors will be considered. It will be seen that a number of changing economic conditions have influenced the change on the North Shore. An attempt will be made to weigh the importance of each of the economic factors.

Elsewhere, in considering the social conditions, a similar delineation and exploration of their ramifications will be attempted. Conditions which appear to be essentially psychological will be treated in still another chapter. Such treatment will be peripheral both because of the very tentative nature of the psychological tenets employed and because of the very limited amount of empirical evidence to support them. But, though this psychologically-oriented analysis has these shortcomings, to conclude this study without it would be to ignore observed situations on the North Shore where uniquely personal rather than social values seem to play primary roles.

The Politics of Preservation

All those who dred uncertainty either because of timidity or from conventional-mindedness or for fear of material loss are enlisted under the conservative standard.

Arthur M. Schlesinger, Sr.

Political power is a basic cause of community change. The influence of politics, first in forestalling, then in precipitating the decline of the Gold Coast cannot be overestimated.

The following discussion will consider the role of politics and the distribution of power in the early maintenance and later destruction of the Gold Coast. It will be shown that both the North Shore estate owners and the American rich, in general, have been losing political strength since the early part of the century — with important consequences. Political power has traditionally been used by the wealthy to maintain social and economic conditions favorable to them. With the loss of political power, it became impossible to prevent the dissipation of many of these favorable conditions. To what extent these social and economic conditions were actually necessary for the preservation of the estate community will be considered in succeeding chapters.

The members of the estate community were heavily involved in politics for they saw it as the means to the desired social and economic ends which they sought. The achievement of many of these goals was held to be essential for the viability of estates and, on a broader level, the Gold Coast. Whether and to what degree these fears were justified are questions that will be reserved for later social and economic analyses. The very fact that these fears existed and that they motivated political involvement is significant enough for the present analysis.

The essential political aim of the estate people was to maintain the status quo, the prevailing system which permitted the ownership of estates in a genuine, upper-class estate area, the characteristics of which have been discussed. To keep the Gold Coast intact, they believed that particular benefits which the system provided were required. An obvious requirement was a sufficient income. Another was a distinctive maximum cost of running an estate. Also, maintaining the character and, thus, the social desirability of the entire area was deemed a requisite. All of these and other felt needs were satisfied in the early part of the twentieth century when the Gold Coast was at its height. The political activities of Gold Coast residents were designed to keep conditions from changing, thereby safeguarding their way of life. At certain times, political activity on one level of government was intensified as a particular threat on that level presented itself. Political efforts were responsible even for creating a new level of government — the estate village.

The present analysis will first consider the modes of political involvement among the wealthy. It will then seek to discover the political mechanisms by which estate people sought to achieve their goals. Finally, the questions of when, why, and to what extent these mechanisms broke down will be analyzed.

DIMENSIONS OF POLITICAL POWER

The political power of the estate people on the North Shore

has had several dimensions. Four general categories are here considered: Voting strength, opinion-making influence, control over public officeholders, and direct control of some government functions by holding office.

VOTING STRENGTH

The voting power of estate dwellers was substantial when the estate community was intact. The large voting block, then as compared to now, exercised solidarity on important issues that might affect their way of life. A more important consideration was the estate employees, most of them qualified voters. It is clear that almost all of these people voted in the same manner as their employers. Estate employees voted in this way for one of two reasons. Often it was based on a sense of identification with the employer and the resulting feeling that whatever was good for the boss was good for them. Other times the vote was cast out of fear. Many an estate owner, it is reported, coerced his employees to adopt his voting preference. As one estate superintendent remarks: "I was told to take the men down and make sure they voted Republican." Election districts were small enough so that general checks were possible on how these decrees were carried out.

The estate people also influenced other local voters, particularly local businessmen and merchants who were heavily dependent on the estates. The economic pressures that estate owners could and did exert on villagers who supported an opposition party or an unpopular issue were substantial. A Cold Spring Harbor plumber of the 1920's spoke out in favor of measures which the estate owners in the area opposed. When he refused to stop, he was prevented from doing work on any estate. Though this particular individual was unusually stubborn and persistent, the economic consequences of his action served to discourage other businessmen from voicing dissent to voting recommendations of estate owners. Besides the political significance in the large number of votes the estate people controlled, these votes were even more politically meaningful since they presented themselves as a solid. block. Because the political interests of the Gold Coast were so homogeneous, the leaders of the area were generally in agreement and collectively directed the votes to be cast in an all or nothing-at-all fashion.

OPINION-MAKING INFLUENCE

The control of public opinion is an important form of political power. This power acts to give popular support in political situations where such support is desired.

Public opinion is shaped through controls and influences on opinion-forming agents, such as newspapers, radio (and, today, television), schools, and churches.

It is evident that the estate owners either heavily influenced or directly controlled such agents on the North Shore and, in collusion with the wealthy in other areas, opinion-forming agents across the country. For instance, Colonel Lloyd Griscom, an estate dweller, reportedly owned several local Long Island newspapers. The support by other local papers came, in part, from pressures exerted by other estate owners. It is clear that the editorial and news reporting policies of these papers were directed by their financial backers. This conclusion is based on examination of local papers and interviews with persons who read them over the years. One such interviewee said, when talking of these papers, "I never saw estate people criticized in any of them."

The rich on the North Shore and elsewhere controlled more than local newspapers. Examples of outright ownership of major papers by the wealthy was common. Marshall Field of Lloyd Harbor owned a major Chicago newspaper, while John Hay Whitney of Manhasset published the popular New York *Herald-Tribune*.

Ferdinand Lundberg, writing in the 1930's, maintained that the entire U.S. press was substantially under the control of the wealthy. To support this, he observed that "happenings of a scandalous tinge relating to persons of great wealth are featured by the newspapers only when the characters concerned obviously desire to have their private affairs written about."[1] The case of Marshall Field II, who was shot in 1906, is an example of this kind of reporting. When Field died, the Associated Press was silent. Only small papers like the *Daily Socialist* of Chicago carried the story.

The rich exerted much influence on churches. The basis of this influence was obviously the very large donations which they made—as true for the North Shore as apparently it was elsewhere. An article in the *Glen Cove Echo* of February 5, 1925 is entitled, "Summer Residents Among Large Contributors to Cathedral Building Fund." This article informs the reader that twelve estate owners (including J. P. Morgan) donated $100,000 each to this project while many others made contributions of $1,000 to $25,000. Aside from the spiritual advantages of this generosity, practical benefit was derived. The author of *The Robber Barons* has discussed the church as an opinion-forming agent: "The Church was to buttress the new regime of status, it was to control, to pacify, to 'render unto Caesar the things that are Caesar's'."[2]

Many North Shore estate owners, among other wealthy persons, gave large sums of money to schools, foundations, and philanthropies. The recipients were either local or national organizations. An example of funds given to a local organization is found in the case of Mr. De Forest of Cold Spring Harbor who helped finance the village library. An illustration of a contribution to a national cause is that of George F. Baker who in 1924 gave $5,000,000 to launch the Harvard Business School. Gustavus Meyers has studied the involvement of the rich in philanthropic work and the personal benefits therefrom. He concludes that philanthropic involvement has given the wealthy tremendous power to shape education and mold public opinion.[3]

CONTROL OF PUBLIC OFFICEHOLDERS

Control of elective offices and of those persons occupying

them is another dimension of political power. This type of power was perhaps the easiest for the rich to acquire and indeed the most effective form of control.

The power to control elected officeholders was initially exercised on all levels of government. The political campaign contribution was the device used to secure it. As a matter of fact, this power varied directly with the size of contributions, assuming that such funds were given to the victorious side. Usually, a contribution was given to each major party. In this way the rich could not lose. The North Shore rich did most of their contributing to national campaigns according to several informed sources. Yet this did not preclude them from "also kicking in on county and town campaigns."

HOLDING OFFICE

The power derived by actually holding public office is the last dimension of political power to be considered. It is apparent that this form of power was largely in the hands of the estate owners. It was most commonly found on the village level of government since here elective positions were little defined and, therefore, the responsibilities of office could be as great or as small as one desired. This flexibility was essential for the Gold Coast citizen in public office due to the great demands on his time made by his business and social commitments.

There are a few cases of estate people holding other than local positions. Mrs. John T. Pratt of Glen Cove, for example, was a Congresswoman. Although some other examples are to be found, most estate people were not attracted to elective positions in other than the village government.

BREAKDOWN IN POLITICAL POWER

The estate people, as we have seen, had each of the four important types of political power. This placed them in a very strong political position. The maintenance of their power was the uppermost concern of these people. They realized how essential this was if their way of life was to continue. They knew this power was their weapon, their only weapon, in the political battles which they had to wage to protect their interests. Some of the conflicts resulted from assaults upon them and, as such, these were purely defensive on their part. In others, the wealthy took the offensive. These were usually initiated to make some aspect of their way of life more secure, perhaps in anticipation of it actually coming under attack. Matthew Josephson in discussing the political involvement of the very wealthy stated: "They were uncommonly eager to have existing private-property rights sanctified and protected by all the authority of the country."[4]

Though the rich were very successful at the beginning of this century in achieving their political goals, they encountered increasingly greater obstacles as time passed. This was symptomatic of their declining political status. This decline resulted from general social and economic trends as well as particular events, and over each the wealthy had no real control. Among the national trends that contributed to this declining political position were the labor unionization movement and the womens' suffrage movement. E. Digby Baltzell in his various studies of the upper class has considered in some depth how these and other historical movements have weakened the rich as a potent political force.[5]

There have also been particular events which have had the result of weakening the authority of the rich. The First World War was one. Throughout our involvement in this world conflict, a federal centralization of government took place. President Wilson had disputes with several business leaders during the war. He fought, for example, with North Shore estate owner Clarence Mackay over the management of the Postal Telegraph Company, of which Mr. Mackay was director. Unable to reach an agreement about "proper" company policy during wartime, Wilson finally put the company under government control until the war's end.[6] The centralization of government for the war effort hurt the rich, for it reduced the channels through which they could exert their influence.[7]

A major event that encroached further upon the power of the rich was the depression. The federal government took the lead in the crisis period of the thirties and again tended to centralize the political power of the country in its own hands.

Also during the depression, the national government provided many programs to give work to the unemployed. Some of the unemployed on the North Shore had worked on estates before the owners reduced their staffs. These persons, no longer economically dependent upon the estate people, felt free to vote according to their own convictions. Loss of voting control, then, was one facet of declining political power among the rich during this period.

With the coming of the Second World War came also added federal control. Such federal centralization of power was damaging to the rich on Long Island as in other wealthy communities. Many of the younger estate employees entered the armed services. Others left the estates for attractive jobs in the defense industries on Long Island which were either established or greatly expanded with entry into the war. Again, loss in aggregate number of estate workers meant loss in voting control.

Shortly after the war another far-reaching development on Long Island occurred which affected estate life. Politically speaking, this changed the complexion of western Long Island.

Until the late forties, there had been only a slow influx of middle-class families to Long Island. As people bought or built homes in an established community, they were assimilated into the local cultural and social system. They adopted the local values and attitudes—and the prevailing political thinking. As one long-time Republican leader states: "They came out of New York City as Democrats and we made them Republicans."

But this process of assimilation broke down in the late forties. In this period of mass development on Long Island, newcomers were not being absorbed in established communities.[8] They were settling in new communities with other newcomers as neighbors. Being physically separated from the old residents, there was little social interaction between the two groups. There were few opportunities to change the generally liberal attitudes of the new group to the conservative thinking of the local villagers and Gold Coasters. This situation, it is claimed, forced the Republican Party to become more liberal in order to compete successfully with the Democratic Party for the new votes. Thus, the statement of a Republican office holder at the time is especially pertinent: "We (the party) changed from a right-wing to a middle-of-the-road party."

The discussion here of the various local and national occurrences which have had some bearing on the political standing of estate owners has pointed to a general political trend. This trend has involved a shift in political power away from the wealthy.

Attempts will later be made to further illuminate this trend and to illustrate its direct and indirect consequences for the Gold Coast. This analysis will involve a review of the major national and local political struggles fought by the wealthy to preserve the Gold Coast as they knew it. Before moving to this analysis, however, consideration needs to be given to a politically-oriented hypothesis to explain the reduction in estate spending in the thirties.

DEPRESSION POLITICS AND WEALTH DISPLAY

In addition to the centralization of government and the other political outcomes of the depression unfavorable for the rich, there is a sense in which the politics of the thirties affected the consumption pattern of the wealthy in an immediate and direct way. One aspect of this relates to how the rich were popularly viewed during this period.

The stock market, although participated in by many small investors, was always thought to be under the control of the wealthy investors and the large investment firms typically headed by the rich. When the crash occurred in 1929, more than a few people were convinced that the wealthy were responsible.

Some even saw it as planned by the rich. It was the common belief of many that the rich always benefited in the panics of the past. Their large capital had permitted them to acquire large blocks of stock during the frantic selling. Huge profits came when the market was restored and stocks returned to their original value.

So it was that many persons came to view the panic of 1929 as intended by and having good prospects for the rich. A contemporary writer expressed his belief that "the ruinous speculative boom that collapsed in 1929 was engineered from first to last, by the wealthy families, and for their personal account." He proceeded to term this whole episode, including the crash, a "politico-financial speculative scandal."[9]

The continuance from the twenties to the thirties of the lavish spending on estates, gala parties, and other items of costly amusement, served to reinforce the suspicions of many. These large outlays of money were particularly obvious because of the low level of spending which characterized the rest of the population at the time. The average person had only to read the papers to contrast the news of increasing unemployment and hardship with the extravagant affairs of the rich. The contrast was so great that sounds of protest among the masses were beginning to be heard.

In January 1931 a debutante party reported to have cost between $50,000 to $500,000 was held in a Washington, D.C. hotel. On the same block, and at precisely the same time, a government relief center was dispensing food to unemployed men and women who formed a long line. This incident disturbed a great many people. The morality of "parties and breadlines" was debated by newspapers, politicians, and a multitude of concerned citizens. Some predicted that a revolution would occur if this continued. Senator George W. Norris of Nebraska pointed out that the same conditions prevailed prior to the French Revolution.

Other persons defended extravagance amid poverty, pointing out that elaborate affairs effectively disseminate money from large accumulations. An attendee of an extravagant North

Shore party of the day recalls numerous conversations at the gala in which the employment which such an event provided was repeatedly lauded. But there is evidence that the majority of Americans were less than fully convinced "that expensive parties serve a useful economic purpose." [10] As one newspaper commentator of the day stated: "The average man, temporarily out of work, bowed down with the support and protection of his loved ones, naturally bitterly resents a vulgar display of wealth. He is not in a frame of mind to analyze the situation and to see that the expenditures which he denounces are not all a total loss." [11]

It remained for Franklin D. Roosevelt to crystalize this growing national concern into a firm political issue. This issue and his position on it was largely responsible for his success in winning public office. Mr. Roosevelt stated the case succinctly when he accepted the presidential nomination: "I pledge you, I pledge myself, to a new deal for the American people." Implicit, and later made explicit, in this, was the goal of ridding "the temple of our civilization of the money changers." Roosevelt affirmed that it was under the system of the rich that the depression came about and assured the American people that, if they followed him, the depression would not only be ended but another one would never occur. Constantly condemning the very rich, he later developed the dichotomy of "the needy" and "the greedy." In discussing the meaning of liberty in one of his fireside chats, he said: "I am not for a return to that definition of liberty under which for many years a free people were being gradually regimented into the service of the privileged few." [12]

Wealthy people began to realize what disastrous political consequences the further display of their wealth could have. With the election of President Roosevelt in 1932, much of the political power of the wealthy was lost. [13] They were no longer in a position to retard or modify political action as dictated by the majority. The distribution of the country's wealth indeed still favored the upper class, but for the rich to give any dramatic indication of this would have caused the situation to change.

In December, 1934, an incident occurred which gave the rich further cause for thought. Income tax statistics were released at this time for the year 1933. *Business Week* reported the data in the following way: "The one million dollar (income) club swelled to forty-six in 1933 against only twenty in 1932. It was the rich that got richer. The middle class lost members and earned less."[14]   Newspapers around the country awarded front-page headlines to this. Most people who had felt that American income levels were converging were most disheartened by the news. The clamor for a redistribution of wealth grew louder.[15]

Many energetic supporters of equal distribution of the country's wealth began to speak out. Huey Long, a southern senator, was such a person. He advocated a "Share-the-Wealth Society" in which no family would have an income less than $4,500 a year. Individuals and groups with similar proposals also began to draw much attention. Pamphlets were prepared and widely distributed by some of socialist-oriented groups. One of these booklets bore the title, "How the Rich Live — and Whom to Tax."[16]

There is reason to believe that a genuine fear took hold of many wealthy people in this period. The political atmosphere had changed. Their common sense told them that the dangers of continuing in their extravagance were too great to chance. They were perhaps beginning to see that "pomp without power paves the way to revolution."[17]

This is one interpretation of the trend toward reduction in spending, at least on obvious luxuries, by the rich after the early 1930's.

POLITICAL STRUGGLES ON THE NATIONAL LEVEL

The political battles waged by the wealthy have taken place on both the local and national front. It is important to consider the major struggles on each of these levels. National struggles were waged by the wealthy in general, while local struggles were the particular concern of the Gold Coast residents. All of these fights were fought to preserve the status quo, the prevailing socio-economic-political system that favored the rich. It is clear that, as political struggles were lost by the wealthy, the changes they feared became inevitable.

Political struggles on the national scene will be briefly considered in the initial discussions. The emphasis will be on the causes of these struggles and the consequences of their outcome.

CONSTITUTIONAL AMENDMENTS SIXTEEN AND SEVENTEEN

Notwithstanding considerable opposition on the part of the rich, the Sixteenth Amendment to our Constitution came into being in 1913. This amendment gave Congress the power to "lay and collect taxes on incomes. . . ." Although this amendment originally resulted in a very small tax, it acted as a wedge, opening the door to heavy graduated taxation which was to come some 20 years later. The rich predicted heavy income taxes and fought the amendment from the time it was proposed in 1909. However, four years later their blocking tactics were overcome.

Another amendment, also greatly opposed by the wealthy, became part of the Constitution in the same year. This was the Seventeenth Amendment which instituted the direct election of senators. Up to this time, senators were appointed by the state legislatures. The appointments were often very much dictated by the wealthy, a source of great political power. In discussing the movements that lead to the passage of the Seventeenth Amendment, Edward S. Corwin and Jack W. Peltason believed that:

> the adoption of universal suffrage and the growing strength of the democratic spirit made it inevitable that United States Senators should be chosen directly by the people. During the last half of the nineteenth century the dissident labor and farmer parties had called for direct election. The revelation of certain senators' great wealth and of their obligations to various large economic interests reinforced these demands.[18]

While the Sixteenth Amendment was economically detrimental

to the American wealthy, the Seventeenth was politically damaging. But these measures were just the first, with more legislative blows to come. The inability of the rich to defend themselves adequately against these attacks demonstrates their declining political power.

MORE TAX REFORMS

It is apparent that many political reform movements of the early twentieth century grew out of the feeling that too much wealth concentration is incompatible with the democratic ideology of equality of opportunity. This was held to be especially true in the case of great inherited wealth. With this national sentiment in mind, Robert J. Lampman states that "to a considerable extent, America's social policy has developed out of the belief that each generation of individuals should stand on its own with a minimum of 'handicapping' by previous generations." [19]

The federal estate tax was authorized in 1916. During the 1920's the income tax was raised significantly. Throughout this time, the rich were busy developing ingenious mechanisms to circumvent these ill-seeming laws. Wills were designated to avoid the inheritance duty, tax-exempt bonds were held to supplement incomes, and a number of other avoidance devices were used in connection with the income tax. The fact that many loopholes existed in the new laws shows that the reform movements fell short of achieving full success. [20]

Many of the loopholes, however, were plugged in the 1930's. A gift tax was established in 1932 and a tax was first imposed on corporation income in 1936. Also during this "progressive" period, the income and estate tax was raised substantially. Some avenues of escape, however, still existed. Trusts could be set up for heirs to reduce estate tax. To lower personal income tax, various techniques were available. A popular device was to incorporate yachts, clubs, stables, and whole estates as businesses and thereby list the amount to operate them as a yearly business loss. This tax evasion method was clearly relied upon by

many members of the North Shore estate community. By incorporating his estate, J. E. Aldred, for instance, was able to
deduct the $100,000 yearly cost of running the estate from his
income. [21]

One author who wrote during the thirties about the weaknesses of tax laws said: "It is safe to predict that when the
New Deal is over the poor will be no richer, the rich no
poorer." The "New Deal," according to the writer quoted, was
not truly progressive. "Some of its tax policies lent color to
the misconception, which will not be eradicated until it is generally realized that the 'New Deal' merely represents an unfamiliar though orthodox way of dealing with problems within
a capitalistic context." [22]

The economic implications of the tax measures will be investigated in a later chapter specifically dealing with economic
conditions. We may observe from our present political perspective, however, that the rich were successful only to a minor
degree in preventing adverse tax legislation from coming into
existence.

OTHER FEDERAL LAWS

Reference will here be made to other federal laws which adversely affected the rich and which they fought staunchly up to
the time of passage.

Estate owners were particularly opposed to the immigration
laws of the twenties. The highly restrictive quota system that
these laws imposed acted to reduce the number of workers who
traditionally were employed by estate owners.

A later law that was passed hurt the rich in a different way.
Directed at political activities, it made it legally necessary for
political parties to publish the size of contributions with the
names of those who made them. Also, maximums were established for these gifts. By making it more difficult for the wealthy
to transform their money into political power, this law took
away from their political strength.

A former North Shore congressman has commented on the impact of this law on the political stature of members of the estate community. To exemplify how much things have changed in the area, he relates a recent experience he had while raising campaign funds through dinners, cocktail parties, and similar functions. Charles D. Hill, a North Shore political leader active in an earlier era, took note of the many efforts that were being made to collect funds. He then said: "Back in the twenties I could raise a million dollars by simply making ten phone calls."

POLITICAL STRUGGLES ON THE LOCAL LEVEL

The political struggles on the North Shore have been many and varied. They have included conflicts with the towns, counties, and state.

More political victories have accrued to the wealthy on the local level than on the national level. This is largely a function of the smaller political base on the local level and the greater ease with which it can be controlled. But, even in this more favorable political arena, a pattern of diminishing political strength of the wealthy becomes evident as their political struggles are chronologically considered.

THE VANDERBILT RACES

In 1904, William K. Vanderbilt, railroad magnate and Gold Coast inhabitant, sponsored the first Vanderbilt Cup Race. This annual auto race, drawing international competition, rapidly became a highly-celebrated American sports event. Hordes of spectators descended on the area to watch. The 1906 race drew 600,000 people.[23]

Jericho Turnpike, a public road on the North Shore, was initially used for this race. Needless to say, this road was not originally built for racing and therefore lacked many features that would have provided adequate safety for the observers. A number of spectators were injured in each race. With the overflowing crowd of 1906, some deaths occurred. It was at this point that the local government, probably after conferring with Vanderbilt, decided to ban the races on public roads. At about the same time, Vanderbilt announced he would build a private road for the races.

Preparation for building the private road, which was to extend from Floral Park to Riverhead, was begun almost immediately with the acquisition of the needed land. Without the benefit of eminent domain, however, such land acquisition proved to be a difficult task. Once the construction began, more unexpected delays were encountered. This prompted a decision by Vanderbilt to continue the races on the public roads until his own was ready. He quickly received consent from public officials. [24]

In the 1910 race, four more spectators were killed and several were injured. National outcries to stop the races followed. In the next session of the New York State legislature the matter was taken up and a law was passed which prohibited races on public roads except with permission of the local government. On October 4, 1910, the Nassau County Board of Supervisors met and, despite great popular opposition, voted to let the racing continue.

This particular episode in the history of the North Shore illustrates the tremendous political power which members of the estate community had. Other early examples of this influence, though less dramatic, can easily be found.

PUBLIC ROADS PRIVATELY ACQUIRED

There is evidence that some estate people whose land either bordered on or stretched out on both sides of public roads, blocked these roads or took them over for their own use and excluded the public. Sometimes alternate routes which skirted the estates were provided by the owners, though even this compensation was not always made.

It is alleged that certain large estate owners who settled in the Cold Spring Harbor area about 1900 were guilty of this action. One public road that was closed by the wealthy was the only public access to the shore. Upon being closed, the beach became inaccessible to the public. This meant that the local residents could not take advantage of the bathing, clamming, and fishing rights that they had.

Several citizens joined together in protest. They demanded that the question of whether this and other roads were public as they claimed should be formally resolved by referring to official maps. But a search for these maps proved fruitless. They had mysteriously disappeared. Without them, the existence of these or any other public roads was impossible to prove.

The group of villagers appealed to the township officials but received no satisfaction. As one of the surviving members of the group has stated: "The politicians always backed the estate people."

"GOLF CLUB" VILLAGES

The term "golf club" village is used to denote a certain type of village that came into existence through the efforts of the estate people. It is a village not in the general sense, but rather in the legal sense. No stores, industry, or conventional residential areas are to be found within their boundaries. Most of these villages do· not have a single gasoline station. They are comprised, rather, of several large estates and often a golf or country club.

It will be seen that these villages were created by estate owners for a few very important reasons. The overall reason why estate owners joined together to incorporate their collective holdings into units of government was to obtain maximum political control on the local level. The immediate reason for incorporating was usually a local political issue of concern to the estate owners.

Before the first estate village came into existence, other communities on Long Island were incorporated. The term "incorporation'' refers to the legal process through·which a community becomes an official village, that is, a self-governing body. Hempstead was the first village in 1853. The next incorporation took place in Sea Cliff in 1883. These and other villages were incorporated so that needed local improvements could be procured. The later estate villages, on the other hand, were incorporated to keep improvements out, for improvements brought both taxes and people to the area. Tax levies and population increases were considered highly undesirable by the estate people.

The first estate village, Saddle Rock, came into being in 1911. The creation of this village, which was made up of a single estate, is an interesting story. Prior to the incorporation, new residents settled in the area around the estate. This meant that public improvements would be needed in the area. Aware of this, the owner of the estate, R. Eldridge, decided he would incorporate his place and provide improvements and services for himself. He realized that the high tax assessment on his estate would mean that he would have to pay a large share of the cost of the major public improvements the town was planning to build. It would be far less expensive for him to set up his own government and provide for his own needs.

Before he could convert his estate into a village, there was a problem he had to overcome. The state law regulating incorporations stated that only an area with a minimum population of 250 people could become a village. Including his family and all his resident employees, there were about 50 people on the Eldridge place. Undaunted, Eldridge proceeded to have a new law introduced in Albany which would change the minimum to 50. Through his substantial political influence, he was not only successful in having the law passed by the legislature but in having the Governor sign it as well.

Having done so much to bring the little village about, it is not surprising that Eldridge was elected its first mayor, nor that his wife was the second person to hold that office. Through incorporation, Eldridge avoided the town road tax, the park district tax, and the water district tax.

A number of estate owners on the peninsula of Sands Point

followed the lead of Eldridge a year later. They carefully drew their village line to exclude all small homeowners. Thus, the southern portion of the village contains the land only on one side of Middle Neck Road while the northern portion includes the land on both sides.

Most of the estate villages were incorporated in the late twenties and early thirties. It was around this time that some of the more densely-populated pockets on the North Shore, such as Oyster Bay and Locust Valley, experienced the creation of many new special districts for water, light, and garbage. The boundaries of these districts were often purposely drawn to include a few estates with very large assessed valuations. The aim of this was to have the few wealthy people pay the greater share of the cost of whatever facilities the new district would provide. This was done despite the fact that many of the estates could not use the new improvements since they operated their own water works, garbage disposal units, and power plants.

The estate people sought the aid of the town to stop this exploitation. But the town could do nothing. If a petition for the creation of a district contained the legally required number of signatures, the Town Board was obligated by law to establish the district. The only alternative was to incorporate. For under the law, a village could not be taken into a special district without its consent.

In addition to avoiding capture into these special districts, the estate owners saw other advantages in being an incorporated area. One advantage was that the town roads in the area automatically became village roads. The decision of improving or widening them was no longer a decision of the town. Such road improvements were certainly not desired by the estate people who sought to keep their area as exclusive as possible. They could now prevent these major improvements from being made. Even basic road repairs like filling potholes could be avoided. With poor roads, travel through the area for the unwary visitor would be difficult, even dangerous.

Another advantage of control of local government was the

power available to pass special village ordinances to further discourage visitors. A favorite law enacted by estate villages prohibited parking on all of the village roads. The estate village of Lake Success, after its incorporation in 1927, passed several laws. One of these forbade swimming in the lake and was enacted "to end once and for all the disturbing Sunday and holiday excursion crowds."[25]

Most of the estate villages had their own police departments. This afforded personalized service (which implies the differential treatment of violators) at a reduced cost. Few policemen are needed in a sparsely populated area. The police force of many villages originally consisted of one man. A small police booth was erected. This structure, as small as six feet square, typically served as Village Hall and Court House as well.

Instead of creating their own police departments, some villages contracted with the County for police protection. The village was required to pay only for the services provided. This was a good economic approach, for the cost to the estate people would have been much greater had they been in the police district and subject to payment of taxes for police service according to the assessed valuations of their properties.

This arrangement gave the Gold Coast low-cost police protection. But this practice ended in the forties. At this time the County decided that, in order for villages to get county police service, they would have to be part of the police district. This development caused a few villages to create their own police departments. Four adjoining villages decided for the sake of efficiency to establish a police force that would serve all four areas.

Before ending this discussion of "golf club" villages, some mention should be made of the procedure by which the estate people were permitted to incorporate their areas, as well as changes in the requirements for this over the years.

Originally it was very simple to incorporate. To do this, all that was required was a small population, a petition with the signatures of a certain number of taxpayers in the designated area, and, finally, an election in which the taxpayers decided whether they wanted to incorporate. Charles E. Ransom, Oyster Bay Town Clerk in the twenties, briefly discusses these elections in an unpublished article he has written:

> During my tenure as Town Clerk I conducted the election in 10 localities to determine whether the area should be incorporated as a village. In most of these villages only a comparatively few home owners were eligible to vote. Under the law the polls had to be opened from one to eight P.M. On several occasions the entire vote was cast in the first hour. However the ordeal wasn't too great. In almost every instance the election was held in luxurious surroundings and the hosts did everything possible to make the hours pass pleasantly. The attorney for the petitioners was usually Winslow S. Coates, an expert in this line. His preparation of all the necessary legal procedures was always thorough and made my task quite simple.

The state law governing incorporations was revised in 1932. This was done specifically to prevent the further establishment of estate villages. The new statute set a minimum of 500 people and a maximum of three square miles in order for an area to incorporate. This could only be an area that was somewhat densely populated. An area made up of large estates could never qualify.

At the time this new law came about, there were still some North Shore estate areas that were unincorporated. It was in this situation that the ingenuity of Gold Coasters again presented itself. A new device was invented to make these areas eligible for incorporation. This was the expansion of existing villages. The new law said only that you had to start with three square miles and said nothing about expanding beyond this. Tested in the courts, the expansion of villages was upheld. Brookville has had a major annexation, Laurel Hollow has had one and Muttontown has had two.

A few unincorporated estate areas, however, did not border directly on a village and so they could not be absorbed by an expansion. In at least one of these areas an attempt was made to create a new village. Colonel Stimpson, a large estate owner in the area, reportedly headed this attempt which took place about 1950. In order to get the minimum population for the proposed village of Sweet Hollow, a densely populated area had to be included. The small home owners who resided in this area apparently didn't care to be a part of a small village and voted the move down in the election.

ROAD-BUILDING BATTLES

In the early 1920's, Robert Moses, then head of the New York State Park Commission, conceived of a plan to have a system of parks on Long Island which would be linked together by parkways. One park in the system was designated for Oyster Bay as a memorial to Theodore Roosevelt. A parkway was envisioned to go from the park to the New York City Line. In its path lay the southern portion of the Gold Coast, the Wheatley Hills estate area. Learning about the proposal, the estate people, according to one close observer, "raised unmitigated hell." The ensuing political battle was a highly complicated one. The struggle is important to consider for it reveals the great political power held by the estate people at that time.

Robert Moses has stated that "Long Island in those days was the wealthiest, most snobbish, and most reactionary community in the United States. The pressure on Alfred E. Smith (then Governor) was enormous." [26] A protest group was formed and funds were raised to oppose the parkway route. It was claimed that the Moses route was unsound and that a route immediately adjacent to the Long Island Rail Road should be used instead.

Several letters of protest were sent to Mr. Moses. "One lady declared that hounds would lose the scent of the foxes when the latter crossed the parkway and that this would spoil the fox hunting. Mr. Moses tried to meet this objection by facetiously proposing underpasses at convenient points to allow the foxes and dogs to get under the parkway." [27]

About the same time this conflict was in progress, a large tract of land became available in Islip on Long Island's South Shore. Mr. Moses immediately sought to acquire this land for another park. But the land was in the vicinity of the exclusive Timber Point Country Club and a few large estates. Some of the wealthy residents in the area felt that a park would discourage new estates near the country club. These people joined with the opposition to the parkway in a general protest against Mr. Moses.

The money needed to buy the park site had to be voted by the state legislature. Because of the great pressure exerted on this body by the estate people, it voted against the outlay. It was only when August Hecksher, a philanthropist and friend of Governor Smith, offered to provide the money that the acquisition was possible. Meanwhile, the parkway proposal was left hanging in air.

In 1929, five years after the route was announced, the opposition remained bitter. The estate people demanded that the route be altered so that it would be about five miles from the estate area. This was finally agreed upon. Under the terms of the agreement, the large estate owners of the area that was spared would pay a combined total of $175,000. The extra cost of the modification to the State and Nassau County has been estimated to be about $2,250,000. Besides the greater cost of construction, the adopted route has presented a five-mile detour to motorists.

In the mid-1950's, a route for the Long Island Expressway was proposed that closely duplicated the originally planned route for the Northern State Parkway. Another protest was heard, but this accomplished relatively little. The only concessions that were made to the estate people were the depressing of the roadway and keeping the number of access roads to a minimum.

The lack of effective opposition in this later confrontation sharply contrasts to the success of the estate owners in the earlier North Shore controversy. It illustrates the reduction in the political power of the North Shore rich.

CENTRALIZING LOCAL GOVERNMENT

Another long political struggle that the North Shore estate

community engaged in was over a proposal to centralize the
government in Nassau County. The proposal was based on a
growing conviction that a more efficient, less costly form of
government was possible for Nassau. It was in 1913 that a committee was set up by the County Board of Supervisors to study
the various possibilities. A full 25 years passed before anything
really concrete came about.

During this period, various committees and groups were
formed which developed outlines for a new county government.
These groups ranged in political composition from partisan, to
bi-partisan, to non-partisan.

It is evident that the estate people wished to avoid any re-
organization of county government. With a more powerful
county government, their own political control would be lessened. With a more efficient county government, the county was
likely to attract more small homeowners. For these reasons the
estate community withheld its support for any specific proposal.

The 1920's was a quiet time for the movement. In the early
thirties, a rebirth of interest occurred. A Democratic Law Committee of Nassau County was created. Its suggested county
charter was described in a published pamphlet *Wonderful Nassau
Wants to Grow*. In the preface of this booklet it was maintained
that "continuance of this ill-suited framework is expensive and
stunts growth." [28]   The proposed charter was designed to centralize government in various ways, including taking away a few
powers of villages. It also would eliminate special districts by
making all of Nassau a single district. A county assessment department was also part of the proposal. At the time, the three
individual townships and the two cities that comprised Nassau
County did their own assessing. Many inequities were alleged
to have occurred under these separate systems. In proposing the
one assessment department for the county, the pamphlet stated
that the assessors "should be free from political pressure and
temptation to assess improperly." Other reforms, including a
master zoning plan for the entire country, were also a part of
the committee's proposal.

The North Shore estate community was quick to condemn

this proposal. It was evident, however, that some form of new government was being demanded by Nassau residents. Realizing this, the estate people tried to influence as much as they could the content of the charter that the people would eventually vote upon. They achieved some degree of success in this.

Under the charter which was finally presented to the voters, the villages that were in existence before the new charter went into effect were to keep substantially all of their powers. Because of the wording of the charter, these powers would actually be protected in the future. A few other features that pleased the estate people were included. Yet the new charter contained some features that were detrimental to the interests of the Gold Coast. It provided for a county assessment department, a county welfare department, and the first county budget.

The new charter also established for the legislative body of the county government (the Board of Supervisors) a new weighted voting system in which the supervisors from the South Shore township of Hempstead would have the heaviest vote. A County Executive, elected by and therefore responsible to all the people in the county, was designated to head the new government.

The general feeling of the North Shore estate community towards this charter was expressed by their vote in the election of 1937 held to determine whether it would be adopted. In the two North Shore townships of North Hempstead and Oyster Bay, the majority of votes were cast against the charter. But an overwhelming majority of votes in favor of the charter in the heavily populated township of Hempstead caused the charter to be adopted.

A new county government, basically opposed by the estate people, therefore came into existence. It was a more powerful county government destined to be controlled by the southern, non-estate sector of Nassau County. The first County Executive was a political leader of Hempstead. In addition, "the new charter brought into being or intensified a 'County Consciousness'." This made the political standing of the estate community even less secure.

LAND-USE CONTROL

In some of the discussions thus far, a few of the methods used by the estate people to discourage either temporary or permanent migration to their North Shore domain have been pointed to. One set of methods not mentioned involved the direct control over land use. These methods were increasingly relied upon over the years.

The "restrictive covenant" was an early device. This was a clause in a deed that stipulated what the deeded property could be used for. Often it read that the estate must remain intact. The use of these conditions of sale to control land use was effective as long as there was full cooperation on the part of the seller. Though the Gold Coaster felt obligated to use this clause when he sold his property, inheritors of estates who were often disinterested in preserving the estate atmosphere of the North Shore had no concern with it.

Until the end of the 1930's, this potential problem didn't bother the estate people. Before this time estates on the market were usually bought by estate seekers. The few estates that fell into developers' hands were usually on the periphery of the Gold Coast. In the late thirties, however, the demand for estates to be continued as estates decreased. Estates were being bought for other purposes.

Measures were needed to halt this trend. It was in this crisis period that the zoning powers of the villages were first seriously used. Before this, the village zoning scheme was a very loose one, not very restrictive. It was essentially a carry-over of the town zoning for the area that existed before incorporation.

The village zoning was now greatly altered. The new zoning laws had two objectives. They were designed, first of all, to insure only estate or large-lot development of land. The second objective was to make estate lands unattractive to developers by greatly limiting the use to which they could be put. Under law, a certain portion of a village had to be zoned for business. To meet this legal requirement, it was common to zone the mayor's front lawn or garden for business.

There was some land that had already been sold before the stringent village zoning was created. Such a tract was the former Harrison Williams estate in Bayville. This 100-acre piece was zoned for houses on 5,000 square-foot lots (50' x 100') at the time it was purchased. Before construction began, the village changed the zoning to require lots of one acre, or about twelve times larger. The firm that owned the land brought suit against the village and was successful in having the new zoning lowered to allow 15,000 square-foot lots.

A somewhat different case of zoning change occurred in the unincorporated Woodbury area around 1940. A building syndicate that had recently bought the Winthrop estate was about to subdivide it. In order to build more houses on the land, the firm sought to have the one-acre zoning changed to one-quarter acre. The Town Board made the requested change. Upon learning of this change, the estate owners in the vicinity strongly protested. This resulted in the Town Board reversing its decision.

During the same period, the nearby Kahn estate was purchased by developers. This building firm similarly managed to have the town downzone the parcel. Despite protest, this decision was upheld. The opposition actually was not as great in this case for the change was only from two-acre to one-acre lots.

As time passed and small-home owners penetrated the estate villages, the control of zoning has often been out of the hands of the estate people. The decisions of these non-estate people with respect to zoning changes has often been protested by the remaining estate owners, but to no avail.

There has also been some difference of opinion among estate owners themselves over proper zoning policy. Estate owners when selling their properties have been notorious for advocating zoning changes that would be detrimental to their estate neighbors. The Pratts of Glen Cove, seeking to dispose of a part of their holdings during the Second World War, obtained a zoning change that allowed them to sell their stables for industrial use. The local political power of the estate people was no longer the solid, undivided, effective force it once was. Zoning changes adversely affecting the interests of most estate people were being made. To become especially common were changes that permitted estates to be used for schools, museums, and other institutional purposes. Examples of these are numerous. After the death of Mrs. Theodore Roosevelt in the late forties, for example, a group sought to take over the Roosevelt home in Cove Neck and operate it as a national shrine open to the public. Many of the residents of the area, particularly the remaining large estate owners, opposed the move. Although some delay in the zoning change resulted from the opposition, the change eventually was made.

Our consideration of some of the broad political struggles of the North Shore estate community has revealed that a gradual weakening of the political position of Gold Coasters has been the general trend. It is essential that this discovery was made before formally treating changing economic and social conditions which are related to the decline of the Gold Coast. Now it may be understood, in a basic way, why the estate community became unable to adequately combat social and economic threats to its existence.

7

Social Conditions and Community Survival

> *... social forces flow with a tidal sweep over communities that are only half conscious of that which is befalling them.*
>
> John Viscount Morley

A number of social conditions have contributed to the change that has taken place on the North Shore. These conditions will be identified and their significance discussed in this chapter.

As with the political conditions previously discussed, social conditions will be found to be either limited to Long Island or so broad as to encompass the entire nation. Two sets of interpretation, the one local and the other non-local, may therefore be developed out of the findings to be presented. The one set would view the decline of the Gold Coast as basically a local social phenomenon, and the other as a non-local one.

Several social conditions will be considered under different subject headings. The first discussion will view the suburbanization of Long Island and the consequences of this for estate ownership. One of the products of this movement, it will be pointed out, has been a change in the image of Long Island and the North Shore. The evolving image is not conducive to

111

estate ownership and has resulted in declining prestige in owning a North Shore estate. The presence of substantial non-estate development in or near the estate area has also resulted in many annoyances for the estate owner.

In addition to the social phenomenon of suburbanization, there have been changes in American culture which have influenced the decline of the Gold Coast. These changes include new attitudes of the non-upper class toward employment as "servants" and new values of the upper class about the most satisfying way of living.

Finally, the characteristics of upper-class marriages and families will be considered. It will here be pointed out that the high divorce rates of many very wealthy people have splintered large capital accumulations that might have been used to maintain estates. The large number of children found in many upper-class families has produced many heirs who have similarly fragmented fortunes.

THE SPREAD OF SUBURBANIZATION

In the discussions thus far, the expression "North Shore estate" has been used. It is now important to point out that this expression was not always as common as it would seem. Fifty years ago estates on the North Shore were referred to as "Long Island estates." Only after Long Island, specifically Nassau County, began to change from a rural to a suburban area was the more specific label adopted. Similarly, it is becoming typical to be even more exact when referring to the location of an estate. Instead of "North Shore estate," one now encounters the expressions "Muttontown estate" or "Brookville estate."

The evolution of this verbal distinction is symptomatic of the changing image of Long Island, the North Shore, and certain communities of the North Shore. To say that one has an estate on Long Island means today something different from its meaning during the first quarter of this century.

Because of the many suburban housing developments that have been created on Long Island, not excluding the northern half, the area's general desirability for an estate has been much reduced. A person, even a highly biased North Shore estate owner, no longer thinks of Long Island as "the social capital of the world." Long Island has become more commonly known as "the bedroom of New York City." The various stages of the changing image of Long Island and the circumstances involved in each will presently be considered.

Transportation on Long Island has had much to do with this. Estate people have always sought to make travel to Long Island, especially to its estate region, a difficult undertaking. They knew that, in the words of a former Long Island Rail Road vice president, "population follows transportation." [1]

Charles Pratt, an early estate owner, had a substantial holding of Long Island Rail Road stock. [2] He was therefore able to influence the policies of the company. Some maintain that he used this control to keep the railroad on Long Island as inefficient an operation as possible. Examples of lack of improvement are most conspicuous on the North Shore. Early in this century the railroad began to make the change to an electrified line. This modernization would make possible faster, more comfortable, and, ultimately, cheaper rail travel. Yet the Oyster Bay branch of the line running through a part of the estate area did not share in the improvement. This neglect was brought to the attention of the railroad company on several occasions, but nothing was done about it. As late as 1942 the company recognized the public response to its failure to act by simply issuing a booklet announcing that electrification would take place sometime in the period 1945-50. [3] Such a plan, however, was not carried out and, in fact, remains unacted upon to-date.

Another proposal for the railroad on the North Shore which the railroad company saw fit not to implement was the connecting of the two North Shore branches to each other. In a 1930 publication entitled, *What the Long Island Rail Road has Done and Plans to do to Improve Its Service—Answers to Questions Asked by the Public Service Commission and Filed*

with the Commission on January 15, 1930, the line made the
following reply to an inquiry of the commission about the
possibility of a future connection: "The company does not
contemplate the construction of a connection between the Port
Washington and Oyster Bay branches because it is not necessary."[4] No elaboration was made.

These various suggestions for the railroad on the North
Shore, if followed, would have significantly improved rail service. Since they were not followed, rail travel remained poor.
Adding to the inconvenience during the early part of this century was the closing in winter of the railroad stations. This prevented these stations from being terminal points for passengers.

Though the absence of rail improvement was most pronounced on the North Shore, the Long Island Rail Road as
a whole was never really progressive. In spite of this, the
railroad has served an increasing number of commuters year
after year. It is significant to note that, while the population
of Long Island tripled from 1900 to 1930, railroad passengers
increased almost ten-fold, from 12.3 million to 118.0 million.
The percentage gain in daily commuters was even greater. The
number of daily travelers rose from 3,700 in 1900 to 87,000 by
1927, a gain of 225 per cent. In the North Shore community
of Huntington, there were only a few hundred commuters in
the early part of the century. At present there are about 2,500.
Similar commuter increases have occurred in other communities
serviced by the railroad.[5]

The railroad, then, played an important role in the development of Long Island suburbia. Though the development of
suburban Long Island began in the early part of the century,
there were restrictions on this growth at the time. "As suburban
residential development took place at first along railroad lines,"
states Long Island transportation expert Charles Stonier, "it
was usually limited to a two-mile radius from the station."[6]
But the "shift from rail to rubber" changed this.

It was about the time of the First World War that the automobile began to be looked upon as more than a means of
sport but as a mode of transportation. Nearness to a railroad

station was no longer a requirement for suburban living with the automobile. Stated in another way: "There were no longer any restrictions of access because of lack of transport." [7]

The population growth of more than a few developed pockets on Long Island resulted directly from the new means of transportation. A true suburbanization movement began. Dr. Stonier comments on this trend:

> ...the increasing mobility of auto, bus, and truck made it possible to "urbanize" large tracts of land which were still essentially rural and which lay between the prevailing transport routes by rail. This progress was held in check only during depression years when there was little demand for new homes, while auto registrations also marked time. But with the large amount of savings accumulated after World War II, it took virtually ten years of expansion to bring supply of new homes in line with demand. [8]

The following account of house-seekers who came to Long Island after the Second World War is given by a Long Island historian:

> Soon after the war was over the roads were jammed every Sunday with people looking for new homes — the war workers who were living crowded into whatever quarters they had been able to find, the returning service men and their brides, older couples who wanted something more modern than the inconvenient pre-war house, families from the city searching for a patch of green lawn in the suburbs. [9]

Before the mid-1950's, large tracts of vacant land and farmland on Long Island had become transformed into residential communities. Levitt, a builder who innovated mass production techniques for erecting small homes, was an important figure in this period. Because of the revolutionary building methods he used, his houses could be sold for prices well below those of competitors in other parts of the New York Metropolitan area. The first Levitt homes constructed were priced under $6,000. A returning soldier, because of the "G.I. Bill," could move in for as little as $100.

By 1948 Levitt had built more than 6,000 houses, with the demand still strong. This demand caused him to build almost twice this number in the next few years before the large parcels of vacant land in the Levittown area were exhausted. Some idea of the tremendous demand for his product can be had by considering that in 1951, when Levitt was completing about 600 homes each month, monthly sales totaled 1,200. Buyers were placed on a waiting list.[10]

Though Levitt's project was the largest, fellow Long Island builders were developing other areas. Long Island was being given a new identity by these men. This was recognized by Long Islanders and non-Long Islanders alike. A college professor on the Island was aware of it as he wrote on Nassau County's history. He spoke of the influx of suburbanites as an invasion and declared that "old families with deep Island roots, some of them living on land which their ancestors purchased directly from the Indians, watch today the incoming tidal wave of young families eager to find homes anywhere."[11]

The change that was taking place on Long Island was common knowledge across the country, largely because of the publicity given it by national periodicals. *Harpers* reported in 1948 on "The 6000 Houses that Levitt Built." It told its readers that "the houses might look quite attractive if there weren't so incredibly many of them." Another passage of the article stated that "a community that, by nature, is limited to families of the same generation from the same income bracket, is potentially a monster."[12] Similar articles appeared in other widely read publications. Even *National Geographic* treated the subject. A general comment found in this publication follows. "Although not on a Levittown scale, hundreds of other housing developments are changing the face of Long Island."[13]

Most of the suburban development took place in Nassau County since this is the closest county to New York City. Between 1946 and 1965, more than 230,000 homes were built here, leaving less than 10 per cent of its 300 square miles undeveloped. Its population of only 55,448 in 1900 rose to almost 1,400,000 by 1967.

TABLE III

NASSAU COUNTY POPULATION, 1900-1965

Year	Population
1900	55,448
1910	83,930
1920	126,120
1930	303,053
1940	406,748
1950	672,765
1960	1,300,171
1965	1,397,727

Source: United Stated Bureau of the Census

Though most of the development has taken place in Nassau County, suburbanization has also occurred in western Suffolk County. Suffolk's population totaled one million by 1967.

As a result of this tremendous development, Long Island took on a new image. It became known more generally as a suburban rather than an estate area. The name of Levitt was becoming more associated with it than the names of its most fabulously wealthy residents. Long Island's changing character reduced the desirability of the Island as a place for an estate.

This reduction in the desirability of Long Island for an upper class residence had two aspects. One was purely social. This is related to the upper-class prescription that members of this group live in exclusive, prestigious areas. Studying this social fact, Zorbaugh finds that "the exigencies of the social game demand that 'society' live in certain neighborhoods."[14]   The North Shore became less identified as such an area when the suburbanization of Long Island got underway. Though this was more pronounced in the sections of the North Shore ·where non-estate development occurred, the social standing of the entire area had suffered by the new image Long Island had gained.

In addition to the influence suburbanization has had in changing Long Island's image and lowering the prestige of

owning an estate here, the relatively high-density development
in the vicinity of estates has caused many annoyances for the
estate owners. One source of annoyance has been the increased
traffic on the public roads at the entrances of estates. This
has reduced both the beauty and safety of the environment.
Many improvements of the roads have been necessary, including
widenings and traffic-light installations. Jericho Turnpike, a
rural two-lane road in the past, is now a busy six-lane highway
in sections. In some heavily-trafficked areas, signal lights have
been placed at the entrances to estates.

The problem of trespassers on estates has become crucial
in many areas. Some trespassers come out of curiosity, without
intention to do harm. Others are outright vandals. A Cold
Spring Harbor estate recently suffered major damage when
one of its structures was set afire. Other notorious trespassers
on estates are hunters. Estate owners complain of them second
only to the vandals. Most of the trespassers do not have de-
structive motives. An estate owner on the fringe of Lattingtown
whose property is near a middle-class residential area reports
that teenagers are continually either walking across the estate
or driving on the private roads it contains. The superintendent
of another estate tells that he is often called upon to chase
couples who "park and neck" on a part of the place. This
occurs both day and night. Annoying episodes involving illicit
entry take place on the great majority of estates, especially
those on the periphery of the estate area. Estate owners in
Old Westbury are reportedly giving serious thought to whether
they should maintain their residences. This area is not only
close to a now densely-populated area, but two rapidly expanding colleges are now situated within its boundary. In addition
to increasing incidents of trespassing, the roads in Old Westbury
have become heavily trafficked. Its residents no longer enjoy
the privacy they once possessed.

Mrs. Harold I. Pratt owns an estate that was one of a
number of contiguous Pratt estates in Glen Cove. She purchased a few of these other estates over the years as they were
about to be put on the market. In this way she has kept her

residence some distance away from the small-home development which threatened to enclose her.

A few other estate owners have also been successful in preventing the development of nearby estates by purchasing them in this way. Landsdale Christy reportedly bought a few of them and held these until the time of his death a few years ago.

But the efforts of these and other estaters have accomplished relatively little in the face of the dramatic change to which Long Island has been subjected. At best, they have served to forestall change in isolated areas. The North Shore has meanwhile lost its general appeal as an area where the multi-millionaire would automatically seek to establish his residence. It no longer has the distinction of being "the smartest place to live."

THE SERVANT PROBLEM—SOCIAL ASPECTS

The "servant problem" has an economic as well as a social dimension. The economic aspect is directly related to the supply of labor. The social dimension concerns the values and attitudes of this pool of labor. A few of the social aspects will presently be considered.

Leaving the question of salary for a later economic analysis, the estate employer-employee relationship of forty years ago will be contrasted with that of today. In the earlier period this relationship was highly structured. The employee occupied a clearly defined position on the estate and knew the functions he had to perform. Supervising him was never the employer himself. That was the responsibility of the superintendent. The employer's orders to the workers were relayed through the superintendent. This was true even if the employer was in their presence. Direct contact was always avoided.

The employees were very respectful of their "master" or "madam." They felt a sense of obligation in serving them. As one oldtimer remarked: "We were proud to serve." Most positions on estates were considered very desirable. There was a lot of prestige, for instance, in being a butler. Perhaps part of this came from the security of estate employment. Employees not only received a constant wage, but were taken care of in time of sickness. Those who held the more important positions could even count on retirement with a continuing income. In return for this highly-sought work, the employees were expected to conform to regulations imposed on them. These rules were often directed at their conduct outside of working hours. Many of the prohibitions had the effect of making the employee entirely dependent on his employer. On several estates, for example, employee ownership of automobiles was prohibited. The practice of requiring household help to be in their quarters by a certain hour in the evening was prevalent. All of these rules were accepted and followed without dissent.

The situation today contrasts greatly with this. Democracy, rather than authoritarianism, is the main characteristic. Employees demand a substantial amount of independence. This is true both on and off the job. After working hours they consider their lives entirely their own. Employer interference is not tolerated. Even on the job employees demand a large degree of autonomy. One estate owner reveals that she has had much difficulty with the girls hired to clean the main residence. They insist, and cannot be dissuaded, from going from one room to another in a pattern they have formulated themselves. Though this pattern presents certain inconveniences at times for the owner, she finds the resistance to change, especially at short notice, too great. Similar management problems are reported by other estate owners. Employees who are energetic and obedient are a rarity.

There is a related problem with the help today. Many workers have a lack of respect for their employers, and they show it. Though this disrespect is usually expressed out of the presence of the employer, it can be embarassing to him. It may involve a criticism of a particular personality trait of the estate owner or a total condemnation of him. The present writer was confronted with this in speaking with many employees. Even the secretary of one "madam," a presumedly personal confidant, exhibited such irreverence. In this instance, the employee described her elderly employer as senile, and did so in a most derogatory manner.

Some of the help are held to be lazy by the employers. Others are found dishonest. One estate couple in Cold Spring Harbor notes that they recently decided to sell their large yacht because they could not find a crew that "could be trusted" to operate it.

There is more direct and informal contact now between employer and employee. This is not because the estate owner wants it, but because the workers refuse to function without it. There are even superintendents talking to employers on a first name basis. A local government official interviewed was recently conducting a land-use survey on the North Shore. This survey involved going from one estate to another and asking questions of anyone available who was familiar with the place. A relatively young superintendent of one estate was being spoken to as the owner and his wife drove into the courtyard. The employee explained the nature of the conversation and the owner nodded in assent. The owner politely reminded the superintendent of a chore that should have been looked after earlier in the day. Thereupon, he drove his car to the rear entrance of the house. The superintendent excused himself, saying that there was a matter he had to attend to. But as he walked away past the owner who was busy carrying his own food parcels from the car into the house, he said to the visitor: "If there is any more information you need, you can ask this fellow." Upon hearing this remark, the employer smiled, turned and offered his assistance to the visitor.

Another example of the more relaxed relationship between employer and employee is presented by Cleveland Amory: "She (Mrs. William G. Holloway of Long Island) has, in the past twenty-five years, been in the kitchen of her 25-acre 'Foxland' just once—and that was some years ago when an accident occurred and the roof caved in. During this era she once had a kitchen maid who worked for her for seven years without even seeing her. In contrast, her daughter-in-law, Mrs. William G. Holloway, Jr., wife of an oil man, had, in her

Fifth Avenue apartment, one at a time, an average of twenty cooks a year, for five years — 'and,' adds the ex-Mrs. Holloway, now Mrs. Denniston Slater, 'I knew them all intimately.' '' [15]

It is evident that estate people would like to continue their relationship with employees in the old tradition. But this is often impossible, for the young employee just does not tolerate it today.

The basis of this change in the employer-employee relationship is the simple social fact that estate work is no longer looked upon in American society as presitgious. It has become demeaning. Young people, especially those trained in specialties such as gardening, do not consider such employment unless they are permitted to dictate their work situation. Without such latitude, they tend to view the work as intolerable.

The changing attitudes of prospective estate employees toward estate work therefore explains the many concessions that estate owners must make to them. Without these compromises, reliable personnel are difficult to procure and impossible to retain. A number of estate owners are fortunate to have employees who have been with them several decades. A few started on the estate when it was established, sometimes over fifty years ago. These workers, most of them superintendents, are no trouble to handle. They are more than happy to work under the arrangement that originally prevailed. The estate people recognize how valuable and irreplaceable these individuals are. George Ferguson, seventy-eight-year-old superintendent of the Mrs. Harold Pratt estate, relates that he attempted to retire seven years ago. He was away for about a year when Mrs. Pratt appealed to him to come back. During the interim period "she had tried many others, but none were suitable."

A sizable number of estate owners have found temporary relief from the domestic help problem by importing foreign girls through employing agents. Under the contracts with them, the workers agree to remain on the estate for a minimum of a year. Most of them leave immediately after fulfilling this obligation. But during their stay they reportedly serve well.

It has therefore become a serious problem to obtain satisfactory help. Some estate owners claim they would "pay anything" for it. But persons that are both willing and able are hard to find.

There is also a problem in getting capable people to perform routine service on estates. According to society leader Newell Tilton, "the only person you can call nowadays who will come quickly and cheerfully is the undertaker."

The servant problem has made operating an estate a difficult and frustrating affair. As one owner put it: "It has become a chore to operate an estate. It is no fun anymore." It can be easily seen how this may well discourage owners and particularly their heirs from keeping the estates in existence. A few people wonder why any estates still remain, given today's servant problem and the many frustrations for those who must face it.

CHANGE IN UPPER-CLASS LIFE STYLE

Another contributing social factor in the reduction in estate ownership on the North Shore involves change in upper-class life style with its implicit new set of values. The values associated with estate ownership are different now. A lavish residence no longer has the same social significance for this group.

Social commentators inform us that "society" is not as it once was. To denote this change, they use the terms "Old Guard Society" and "Cafe Society." The latter, the newest version of the upper-class theme, is far less formal than the "Old Guard Society." The earlier formality that characterized society involved close conformity to prescribed ways of behaving (mannerisms) as well as the possession of certain physical items. These commodities ranged from fine clothes to a country estate. The degree to which one was successful in obtaining these served as an index of social standing.

The distribution of prestige among the upper class today, it is maintained, no longer operates in this way. This material basis of status, so much a part of the Protestant ethic, has given way to other status indicators. Before considering in more detail the implications of the current life style of the rich for estate ownership, it is noteworthy to discuss what has brought it about.

More money in the hands of the non-upper class today has meant that the show of wealth does not command the attention it once brought. Veblen spoke of "pecuniary emulation" and identified it as the objective of lavish spending by the rich.[16] As money became available to many, this type of emulation was reduced. Amory considers this and concludes that the current rarity of huge outlays by the wealthy for expensive parties and other costly amusements is due "not so much to the fact that too few people have money as that too many do."[17]

Another fact involved in the changing life style of the rich is the mass production and general distribution of once-scarce luxuries. Two commodities, in particular, once available to the privileged few, have since become obtainable for all. These are fashionable clothing and the automobile. At one time each of these was a mark of high social status. Now, almost everyone owns them.

Leisure is another item that all seem to have today. This has resulted from the trend of shorter work hours for the masses. A life of "conspicuous leisure" had traditionally been associated with a member of the upper class. But this status symbol virtually disappeared as leisure became widespread.

The mass media also played a part in changing the characteristics of the upper class life. Not too long ago, the rich actually had a distinct subculture of their own. This included a vocabulary of special terms. The mass media has diffused this to a great extent. It has given the country a mass culture. Social classes have been brought closer together as the cultural differences among them have substantially disappeared.[18] Mass education, another recent development, has certainly accelerated this change.

Through the influence of the social trends cited, the life style of the wealthy has been altered. It is closer now to the style of living of the middle class. The emulative process, we noted, is in part responsible for this. Perhaps more important are the mass social characteristics of society which have emerged. In this social atmosphere, class consciousness has been largely replaced by mass consciousness. The need for status markers, as the ownership of a big estate, is no longer felt to be that great.[19]

Some other factors accounting for the changing mode of living of the wealthy should be mentioned. Included here are the rapid transportation advances which have recently been made, especially in the field of air travel. It is now possible to fly from one large city to another in a very short time, even if they be separated by an ocean. Many moneyed people are apparently taking full advantage of this. They enjoy staying for brief periods in places all over the world rather than confining themselves to a particular locale. An estate is viewed as an encumbrance. If they are to own residences at all, these are typically many in number, small in size, and situated in their favorite resort spots around the world. As mentioned in an earlier chapter, North Shore estate owners of 50 years ago also had more than one residence. But these people spent a considerable portion of the year in each residence. The new wealthy, in the words of one elderly estate owner, "jump back and forth." In the words of another old timer, "they hop around from place to place." Little time is spent in any one place by many young wealthy persons today. They are part of the "jet set."

A final causal connection is apparent between the Second World War and the changing life style of the rich. During this war, the estate owners on the North Shore were obliged to make certain sacrifices. Many of these resulted from the rationing system of distributing household supplies. This forced estate owners to live on a scale greatly below that to which they were accustomed. A few actually closed the main residence and lived in a more modest dwelling on their places. Another adaptation device in this period was to shift garden activities from the creation of flowers to the cultivation of vegetables. By the war's end, some estate owners found that they were quite content with the life style that they had adjusted to and they decided to adopt this new routine.

There have, therefore, been many factors responsible for the change in upper-class life style. This new mode of living, as noted, provides little incentive for the wealthy person to own an estate. A recent newspaper article discusses the lessening attraction of estates as residences for wealthy individuals. The title of this article is "Big Estates Passé Among Rich."[20]

FAMILY CHARACTERISTICS OF THE VERY WEALTHY

Conclusions about upper-upper-class marriage and the family to be presented below, will serve as the basis for an economic hypothesis to be developed in the next chapter. This economic hypothesis will explain the reduction in ownership of costly country estates as a product of the splintering of large family fortunes. Although, as will be noted, this splintering is partly due to certain tax laws, especially the graduated inheritance tax which has encouraged diffusing wealth among inheritors, also responsible are sociological variables. These factors are concerned with the structure of the upper-upper-class marriage and the family. By examining the features of each, it will be seen how these militated against keeping large fortunes intact.

The divorce rate, first of all, appears to have been higher for the upper-upper class than Americans in general.[21] It is difficult, however, to find good statistical evidence of this. A number of very wealthy individuals, among them one-time North Shore estate owners, could be pointed to and the many marriages they have had could be traced. Multiple divorces have been common, for example, with members of the Wool-worth-Hutton family, of which Barbara Hutton is a member. Divorces in other North Shore families have also been very frequent. August Shirer, superintendent of the Bonney estate in Upper Brookville, has made notes in a looseleaf book of most of these local divorces over the last few decades. It is now a large book. In undertaking this, Shirer has closely examined the society pages of newspapers and extracted the desired information.

Social commentators of the rich have also been aware of the short marriages which seem to be prevalent among members of this group. Amory, treating this under the broader heading of morals of the very wealthy, concludes that there has been a gradual movement on the part of the upper class from the old double standard to no standard at all. Divorce, he maintains, is the rule here rather than the exception. The debutante, according to Amory, can expect two to three husbands during her lifetime. He speaks of men, meanwhile, as periodically going through a "change of wife." [22]

One of the few statistical studies which provide support to generalizations of this sought was done by Pitirim Sorokin in 1925. Sorokin gathered statistics on a little over 600 American millionaires and multi-millionaires. He found that their divorce rate was twice as high as that of the average American. [23]

Admittedly, neither the Sorokin survey nor the statements of close observers of the upper-upper class are adequate proof that this group has a high divorce rate. But, since there is no evidence to the contrary, at least the possibility of this high rate must be recognized. Even if the divorce rate of the upper-upper class has been no higher than the rate for other social classes, the mere fact that divorces are not uncommon here permits us to make the point (to be later developed) that divorces have contributed to the break-up of large family fortunes. Even among the not so upper-class today a common remark made, when a divorce is brought to someone's attention: "I didn't know he was doing that well!," thereby associating divorce with wealth.

The composition of the upper-upper-class family, particularly in the number of offspring, is another important social item to consider. The Sorokin study revealed that the rich have generally had large families. He found that his sample family had over four and one-half children on the average, while the 1920 federal census showed that the typical American family had a little over four. Sorokin recognized that his finding conflicted with the general tendency that the number of children in a family varied inversely with the level of family income. His conclusion was, although lower fertility seems to exist among higher-income groups, this is not so for the wealthiest who seem to feel no economic necessity for artificially controlling their offspring.

Ralph Thomlinson, in a modern volume, discusses current studies of upper-class fertility. He concludes that a relatively high birth rate exists among exceedingly affluent families. [24]

This discussion has pointed to the possibility of the upper-upper-class marriage being a relatively brief and frequent experience, while the yield of children as being relatively high. Both this divorce rate and birth rate have had ill consequences for the maintenance of family fortunes. The break-up of a marriage, as will be shown, is a costly ordeal for the wealthy partner, while the proliferation of children results in the multiplication of heirs.

The Economics of Change

He who will not economize will have to agonize.
Confucius

Economic considerations must be given high priority in an interpretation of the decline of the Gold Coast. There is substantial evidence that the continuing disappearance of the great estates is significantly influenced by economic factors. The analysis of the economics of change on the North Shore has been delayed to this point because economic considerations are often the product of political and social conditions. It has therefore been more appropriate to consider these two sets of factors first.

The economic interpretation of North Shore change is not an uncomplicated matter and cannot be simply stated. However, the tendency in some other analyses of the decline has been to so simplify. Many casual observers, among them newspaper writers, have treated it in the simplest of terms. The result has been shallow analyses that are both incomplete and distorting. In the present effort, economic conditions will be closely examined before an estimate of their influence on change on the North Shore is made.

One of the conclusions reached in the previous chapter was that the social advantages of owning a North Shore estate became continually less over the years. Among the themes that will be developed in this chapter is that, from an economic standpoint, this benefit of estate ownership has become more and more costly to obtain.

The increasing economic strain in owning an estate has three sources. First, the operating and maintenance costs of estates have been rising. Second, the economic standing of estate owners as determined by income and accumulated wealth has been declining. Finally, North Shore land has been increasing in value to such heights that the alternative of selling estate land rather than keeping it is very attractive.

SPIRALING COSTS OF ESTATE OWNERSHIP

There is some difference of opinion over whether it is really economically more difficult to keep a North Shore estate today than it was in the early part of the century. Though most estate owners maintain that it is, a few claim otherwise. Because of the lack of adequate data, the argument is impossible to resolve conclusively. The following discussion will present opposing viewpoints and critically discuss some of them. It is clear that the most popular view, and the most convincing one in the light of our evidence, is that owning and operàting an estate has become an increasingly expensive proposition.

THE SERVANT PROBLEM – ECONOMIC ASPECTS

In a section of the previous chapter which concerned the operation of an estate, it was pointed out that a great many workers were needed to keep a large place going. It will now be seen that these workers, because of various social and economic reasons, came to be obtainable as years passed only at very much higher wages.

Before the First World War the cost of estate labor was quite low. Both skilled and unskilled workers were typically immigrants, some having been imported specifically for particular estates. These individuals, as well as a few Long Island natives, were only too happy to have the steady employment which an estate provided. They could be procured at nominal salaries. A common laborer might receive as little as $1.25 a day.

The labor picture changed in the 1920's. Many employment opportunities existed which reflected the prosperity of the nation in this decade. With the increased demand for labor from other sources, the estate owners were forced to raise salaries as an incentive for their help to stay. The regular laborer was paid as much as $4.00 to $5.00 a day. The higher wage was established as more than a response to heightened labor demands. The decreasing supply of labor was another factor. After 1924 the native labor pool was no longer greatly supplemented by immigrants, for in this year a highly restrictive immigration law was passed.

The trend in the 1920's of increasingly better wages for estate personnel did not continue into the 1930's. The reduced economic activity of the nation and its corollary of fewer employment opportunities were contributing factors. A large segment of the labor force came to be unemployed during these times. In this situation, there was no problem obtaining people to fill estate positions, and to have them do so at wages which were no higher than during the twenties. As a matter of fact, a number of owners found that they could reduce salaries and still not be at a loss for people.

The Second World War disturbed this very agreeable labor situation. Not only were many men taken off the labor market by the armed services, but also the demand for labor to make the materials of war increased. A number of Long Island firms were among those given hefty defense contracts. Their payrolls soon mushroomed and Long Island quickly became noted as the center of the aircraft industry.

Some aircraft companies began on the Island a few years

prior to the war. During the war other firms moved to Long Island from the city to expand. Included among these was the Sperry Gyroscope Company. The war, with its great need for aircraft and parts, gave a tremendous boost to such companies. Starting with 1,000 employees at the beginning of the war, Sperry was employing 32,000 at its end.[1] Grumman Aircraft Engineering Corporation and Republic Aviation Corporation were other major wartime employers on Long Island.

The war, therefore, increased the demand for labor while it reduced the supply. This meant that the estate people had to raise salaries significantly in order to secure workers. The wages offered, moreover, usually had to be higher than those obtainable elsewhere. The changing values toward estate work began to emerge during this period. Jobs in the war industries were considered more attractive than estate work. By offering just equal salaries, the estate owners could not successfully compete for help.

The labor situation did not improve for the estates after the war. The employment opportunities accompanying the suburbanization of Long Island substituted for the defense jobs that were obtainable during the war. Work in construction was particularly available as numerous residential communities were being developed. The major housing developments were begun in the late forties. Building activity remained intense throughout the fifties. During that decade more than 147,000 single-family homes were built in Nassau County.[2] The number of men needed for the various projects was substantial.

Jobs in manufacturing, although cut at the war's end, increased on Long Island over the years. Large federal defense contracts awarded to Long Island firms were, in part, responsible. Also, new firms outside the defense industry were established on the Island. Some of these relocated from New York City to obtain the land needed for expansion. Many of the manufacturing firms became very successful and increased their employment significantly. By 1966 jobs in manufacturing on Long Island had reached 144,500. The average weekly salary was $114.52.[3]

In addition to the workers required by the growing building and manufacturing industries, many employees were needed in the service industries. Dr. William L. Leonard, in an article entitled, "Economic Aspects of Suburbanization," points out that "it is a well-known economic fact that because of re-spending, every job in manufacturing and construction (secondary area) generates jobs in the tertiary area, that is, in transportation and utilities, in distribution, in household, business and financial services, in entertainment, education, medicine and other professional services, and in government." [4] Competition for estate workers grew especially keen as a result of these new service industries. Many of the commercial service areas demanded the same kinds of workers that were needed on estates. Gardeners, for example, were required by nurseries which sprang up to serve the suburban homeowner. They were also demanded for maintaining the grounds of the more affluent newcomer whose residence was often on a one- or two-acre plot. For unskilled laborers, maintenance jobs in industry or government became available. This employment surpassed estate work in job security and wage structure. An Upper Brookville estate owner tells how he must compete for labor with the nearby public school which starts maintenance men at $100 a week.

The suburbanization of Long Island has therefore resulted in many local employment opportunities for skilled and unskilled persons. In order to obtain the people needed to operate an estate, owners have had to provide salaries at least commensurate with the going rates. This is as true for chauffeurs and cooks as it is for people to take care of the grounds and clean the house. Mentioned earlier was the practice of importing domestic servants. Such people can be obtained for the cost of their transportation and the payment of an agent's fee. They are paid at a rate not exceeding $150 a month and, according to the conditions of the contract, the employer is guaranteed service for a minimum period, commonly one year. Yet even this wage is three times the salary of domestics thirty years ago. The present salary of domestics who are not employed through the importation method is often as high as $300 a month. Though the wages that must be paid are higher, some estate owners see advantages in employing girls from this country's labor market. Greater permanency of service is just one advantage.

Chauffeurs and cooks are obtainable only by offering salaries far exceeding former wages. Attempts are made to attract couples to serve on estates, the female partner to act as a cook and the male to be a chauffeur or fill some other key estate position. The demand for these couples is so great that high salaries are being offered to them. There are current cases of offers as high as $1,000 a month.

Obtaining common laborers for an estate, as indicated, has also become a serious problem. Estate owners must often pay wages approaching $100 a week. Only thirty years ago, six workers could be had for this amount. On some estates today, laborers who do exactly the same work receive different salaries. This device is used by owners to procure employees at a minimum salary acceptable to each. Certain personnel difficulties have resulted from this policy. If a worker discovers that his peer is making more than he is, he will experience "relative deprivation" and may seek compensation in illegitimate ways. He may resort to theft or may become relaxed in the performance of his duties.

The facts reveal that the growing labor problem has been a definite source of increasing economic strain for estate owners. Some estate people, however, suggest that the labor problem is not as severe as it seems on the surface. They maintain that the expenditures of estate owners on labor are no more than what they had been. Far fewer workers, it is claimed, are needed today on an estate because of the availability of mechanical aids. In one interview on an estate, a long-time superintendent pointed to a row of large trees on each side of an estate road and explained that these trees were almost as big when they were moved into that formation from various parts of the estate about forty years ago. In undertaking this task, only horses, men, and hand tools were used. The principal function of the men (about thirty of them) was to dig the deep holes for the trees. Today the same job could be performed with only a handful of men and two or three specialized machines. Other estate jobs are also greatly facilitated with modern equipment. Cutting the grass on a large estate, for example, is now quickly done by a single man driving a tractor pulling a grass-cutter attachment. Such mechanization illustrates how much greater the output of an estate worker is today compared to what it was years ago.

Notwithstanding these examples, it still seems that an estate owner today must spend more on labor if he wishes to maintain his estate in the early tradition. There are estate jobs like those in the greenhouse where few labor-saving devices are applicable. These and other tasks require human industry equal to that needed in the past.

OTHER OPERATING COSTS

Besides increased outlays for labor, other estate expenses have risen significantly over the years. Among these expenses are those of gas and oil for the several heated buildings on an estate, especially the main residence. The main house is a large consumer of heating fuel with its many rooms. These rooms, in addition to being numerous, are exceptionally large with high ceilings. They were built this way because air conditioning units were not available at the time of their construction, and this was the only way to keep a house cool on warm days. With the higher cost of fuel today, heating a mansion and other estate buildings has come to represent a large expense.

The great consumption of fuel for heating is due to more than the number and size of the rooms. It also results from the now old and antiquated heating systems that these mansions have.

A few estate owners have tried to reduce their fuel bills by undertaking major improvements to make their homes more efficient. At least one individual has razed the old residence and has replaced it with a new one on the same site. This has been done by an owner of a 400-acre estate in Oyster Bay Cove. His modern home replaces a structure that was three times larger and far less economical. Though operating expenses can be cut with major improvements, substantial capital outlays are needed to accomplish this.

MAINTENANCE OF ESTATE STRUCTURES

Keeping estate structures, especially the mansions, in serviceable condition is another increasingly costly aspect of ownership. These buildings, most of them over fifty years old, are constantly in need of repair. Though these buildings were constructed carefully and with the best grade of materials, time has taken its toll. They now must undergo regular maintenance if they are to continue to perform their originally intended function.

The cost of this care is substantial. It would not be so expensive were only ordinary maintenance required. But these estates were not built as ordinary residences. Established as pleasure properties, the buildings were given remarkable detail. Many of their appendages were either hand-carved, hand-wrought, or were produced by some other non-machine operation. Similar craftsmanship is called for to maintain these structures properly. Such fine workmanship today is extremely costly.

When the buildings have been neglected for awhile, extensive refurbishing is needed to make them livable. This is an expensive proposition. Even more costly is an attempt to go beyond merely bringing the structures out of disrepair and to restore them authentically. To gain an idea of what is involved in this restoration, consider the work that was recently completed on the old Theodore Roosevelt estate house on Sagamore Hill in Cove Neck. When it was taken over by an historical society in 1949, it was found to be in need of extensive overhauling. The cost of the work amounted to $200,000. This residence contained just 26 rooms, a small structure compared to the main dwellings found on other estates.

PROPERTY TAXES

The taxes on a North Shore estate have risen dramatically over the years. This, as we shall see, is due to more than the increased cost of operating a local government. It is related to the expansion of government and the great proliferation of its services.

Discussed earlier were some of the political devices used by estate people to preserve low real estate taxes. These included several owners joining together and forming a village for the purpose of keeping public improvements and costs away from them. But it was found that with the reduction of political power of the estate owners, these devices to prevent change broke down.

Areas that were originally comprised solely of estates needed few public services. The estates, it has been pointed out, were self-contained operating units. They had their own water supply, garbage disposal units, and facilities to fill other needs. Little police protection was needed in these sparsely-populated regions, since all estates employed their own armed guards.

When smaller residences were established on Long Island in the estate areas, the situation changed. The owners of these small homes, though they might have as much land as a few acres, were not equipped to provide their own services. They had to rely on public agencies for these.

The newcomers demanded all sorts of government services and improvements. It seemed to one public official interviewed that "they wanted everything." Certainly this impression is supported by the wide spectrum of government activity petitioned by the new residents. Major improvements sought ranged from public pools to public schools. A host of services from fire protection to garbage collection were similarly requested. Nor was the new sentiment only to increase the quantity of these services — the goal was to raise their quality as well. The estate people had little concern with the quality of public services. They cared little, for example, about improving the public school systems. These schools served the children of the estate workers and

villagers, rarely those of the estate owners. The latter attended
private boarding schools. The new suburbanites who came to
the estate areas, however, did not usually plan a private education for their children. They were therefore concerned with
raising the standards of the public schools.

Suburban growth brought a need for more police protection.
It is interesting to note that the need for police protection increases more than proportionally with an increase in population
density. Police service is expensive to provide.

These were among many items that came to be demanded of
the government. In order to provide these services and improvements, tax rates on properties had to be set increasingly higher.

J. E. Aldred, who established a $3,000,000 estate in Latting-
town, paid a real estate tax of $2,000 in 1916. By 1942, this
had risen to $25,000.[5] It is not unusual for a comparably as-
sessed estate today to be taxed in excess of $50,000. Current
assessment records show that estates vary quite a bit in the
taxes their owners must pay. This is mainly because the acreage
and facilities of estates differ so greatly. Thus, the 1967 taxes
of the elegant Merle-Smith estate in Cove Neck were about
$25,000, while those of the larger and more elaborate Winston
Guest estate in Brookville amounted to more than $59,000. The
most heavily-taxed estate today is that of John Hay Whitney
whose several-hundred-acre residence in Manhasset is taxed
annually at almost $143,000.

Even in estate areas where little small-home development has
occurred over the years, taxes on estates have continued to rise.
Two factors are responsible for this tax increase. With the trend
of many estates being taken over by public or non-profit organizations, the tax base (i.e., total assessed valuation) of estate
regions has become increasingly smaller. This means that, to
keep government revenue from decreasing, the remaining tax-
able properties must be more heavily taxed. When estates are
converted to institutional uses, moreover, local government
services, especially police protection, must increase for them.
Because of the decreasing tax base and the increasing need for
public services in estate villages where institutions have been

located, some estate owners have recently proposed a state law to give them tax relief. One tax relief method that has already been used is the "tax phase out." This had recently been used by New York State when it acquired the 1,700-acre Lloyd Harbor estate of Mrs. Marshall Field. It involved paying the village of Lloyd Harbor decreasing yearly amounts over a five-year period as compensation for removing this large holding from the tax roll.

A recent cause of increase in estate taxes in Nassau County occurred four years ago when the County government passed an ordinance ordering the reassessment of all vacant land. The new assessment for vacant parcels was often more than twice as high as that of the old one. Much of the vacant land that was reassessed was part of estates. Thus, the new law acted to increase the taxes on many estates.

Though estate property taxes have moved upward over the years to their present high level, some owners point out that this is not as economically detrimental as it seems. For this expenditure is completely deductible on one's income tax. This means that if a person is in the 70-per-cent-tax bracket, as many estate owners are, a real estate tax of $30,000 represents only a $6,000 personal outlay. Yet the many estate owners who have retired from business and live off accumulated wealth, rather than yearly incomes, do not get this relief.

The consideration of four traditional estate expenses has revealed that the cost of owning a North Shore estate heightened since the early days of the Gold Coast. The extent to which this became an economic strain to the owners is dependent upon these persons' economic status — their ability to afford this. Before owning an estate can be listed as an economic burden, therefore, a view of changes in the economic status of owners is necessary.

DIMINISHING PERSONAL WEALTH

In this section will be considered changes in the general eco-

nomic standing of estate people throughout the history of the
Gold Coast. It will be seen that this standing was reduced for
many during this period.

There are two items that determine personal economic position. These are income and accumulated wealth. The evidence
to be presented reveals that each of these has declined for the
very wealthy. When considering this decline in conjunction with
the earlier finding of rising costs in owning an estate, it must
be concluded that the ability of these people to afford a North
Shore estate has greatly lessened.

INCOMES

Trends in income of estate owners are particularly important
to consider in connection with the increased burden of estate
ownership. There is evidence that it was the original intention of
estate owners to use merely a portion of their regular income,
and no more, to maintain their North Shore residence. The
thought of dipping into savings for this purpose did not occur
to them. Often, even major improvements were made without
resort to one's stored wealth. One individual, Bertram Work,
it is reported, acquired a small estate site in Mill Neck and, in
discussing a main residence with an architect, said that he wanted its cost not to exceed his annual income. That income, he
stated, was approximately $300,000.

Since estate owners in general did not spend more than they
earned due to their reluctance to tap their savings, let us look
at trends in the average income of the very wealthy and regard
it as an important economic variable.

The money made each year by any wealthy individual, as
well as by any other American person, was completely his own
until 1913. In that year, a constitutional amendment introduced
the first permanent personal income tax. Although this tax was
very small in the beginning, it caused an immediate reduction
in the estate owner's disposable income. Some wealthy individuals reacted to this by feeling that they would have to lower

personal spending. A daughter of Walter Jennings, former owner of a 350-acre estate in Lloyd Harbor, recalls a discussion between her mother and father on the day the income tax was made law. Mr. Jennings began the talk by announcing: "We're going to have an income tax." His wife, puzzled, asked exactly what this was. He informed her and added: "We will have to cut back on some spending."

During the prosperous 1920's, high incomes appear to have more than offset the small income tax. Likewise, because of big earnings, the increased cost of labor during this period was not a real burden to the estate people.

The next development to have a bearing on income levels was the stock market crash of 1929. The connection between this event and change in estate owners' incomes is not altogether clear. It is apparent that those persons who derived much of their earnings from stock manipulations were hurt very seriously by the market collapse. A close friend of large estate owner Clarence Mackay relates how Mackay purchased a large block of stock recommended to him by J. P. Morgan and Company in August of 1929. Mackay planned to sell the stock he had at the time, but decided to wait out a lull in the market. When the crash came in October, he still owned both huge blocks of stock.

The Mackay case, however, seems to be untypical. The fact is that most people who relied upon the stock market as a principal source of income were persons of moderate wealth, not the Gold Coasters. The latter had their money invested in many different areas, both in this country and abroad. With such diversified income sources, the crash brought very few of them close to ruin.

In the great depression of the thirties triggered by the crash, there were indications that many high incomes were reduced. These incomes were derived from the profits of the large businesses the rich controlled.

As the depression deepened, the profits from even successful enterprises declined.

There are varying estimates as to how much the incomes of

the wealthy were lowered during this period. Lundberg has estimated the reduction to be between 25 and 50 per cent.[6] Limited data are available to obtain a more precise idea. Internal Revenue statistics are valuable. Based upon them, the following table has been constructed which shows the number and distribution of incomes over $1 million in 1929 and in 1932.[7]

TABLE IV

INCOME OF ONE MILLION DOLLARS OR MORE
IN 1929 AND 1932

Net income in million dollars	Number of persons earning this in the United States	
	1929	1932
1 − 1.5	234	12
1.5 − 2	123	3
2 − 3	67	3
3 − 4	32	0
4 − 5	19	2
over 5	38	0
Total	513	20

These statistics indicate that the number of incomes of a million dollars or more were 96% fewer in 1932 than in 1929. It may be assumed that the incomes of persons who made less than a million dollars before the depression similarly dropped during the depression.

In order to adjust to their lower incomes, many estate people sought to reduce estate expenditures. Efficiency experts were often hired to develop proposals aimed at saving the estate owner money. The various suggestions ranged from cutting the number and salaries of help to being more conservative in the consumption of estate supplies and services. George Elwood, a Cold Spring Harbor plumber who did much work for estates, tells that, when the depression came, the owners asked him to do only jobs which were absolutely essential. Repairs averaging $3,500 a year on an estate before 1929 were reduced to as little as $500 after this year. And bills presented to owners were scrutinized for the first time.

A present executive of Harder Exterminating Service recalls the state of his business during the thirties. At that time, more than 90 per cent of its customers were estate owners. The informant tells that these clients would freely spend money only during periods when the national economy seemed to be improving. "Our business was always better when the stock market was rosy," he states.

There are some observers who believe that the incomes of many estate people suffered little in the early thirties. They point out that a number of estate owners did not reduce spending during this period. Indeed, there are examples of increased activity on some estates. Harold Pratt of Glen Cove, for instance, hired additional personnel to work on special projects to enhance his estate. Many owners made no reduction in the number of employees or in the amount of their salaries.

The case of the estate-serving business district and residential community of Westbury during the depression illustrates that estate expenditures, at least of estates in this area, may have changed little during this period. Residing in this village were many people employed on the nearby Wheatley Hills and Old Westbury estates. Also located here were several small businesses that depended substantially upon the estate trade. The economy of this village, measured in terms of employment and success of businesses, was very good during the depression. This contrasted to the poor economic condition of communities to the south which had large commuter populations.

If it is true that there were estate owners who did not curtail spending during this period, it must be recognized that this may not have been due to unchanged earnings. There is evidence that some owners had a lower income yet still maintained their traditional standard of estate living. These people spent more than they earned and thereby lived off their capital. Those who did this were, for the most part, elderly estate owners who did not anticipate living for a great many more years.

Although Internal Revenue statistics show that the number of people in America with very high incomes was small during the depression years, the available data reveal that this high income group grew with members in later years. The table below lists the number of income tax returns of one million dollars or more in the pre-depression year of 1929, the depression year of 1932, and various post-depression years. Population data is also provided to show that the growth in the number of people with million-dollar incomes increased after 1932 more than proportionately to our expanding population.

TABLE V

UNITED STATES POPULATION AND NUMBER OF INCOME TAX RETURNS OF ONE MILLION DOLLARS OR MORE* IN THE UNITED STATES

Year	Income Tax Returns of a million or more	Percentage Change	Total Population add (000)	Percentage Change
1929	513		121,770***	
1932	20	− 96.1	124,840***	+ 2.5
1944	62**	+210.0	138,916***	+11.3
1950	219**	+253.2	152,271	+ 9.6
1960	306**	+ 39.7	180,684	+18.7
1964	482**	+ 57.5	192,120***	+ 6.3

*This is income before taxes and after business expenses.
**These include individual as well as joint returns.
***These are estimated totals.
Sources: Internal Revenue Bureau of the United States Treasury Department and the Census Bureau of the United States Department of Commerce.

This table reveals that the number of incomes of one million dollars or more has increased substantially since 1932. However, the number of such incomes in 1964 (the latest year for which data is available) still fell below the total recorded in 1929.

Up to this point, consideration has been given only to net income. With a very small income tax before the early 1930's, gross earnings were very close to disposable income. This was not the case after 1932. Even a year before Roosevelt took office, Congress revised the income tax law to make the portion of one's personal earnings over $100,000 taxed at a rate of 48 per cent, replacing the rate of 20 per cent established in 1928.

In 1934, 1935, and again in 1936, this levy was substantially raised by President Roosevelt. Before the end of his administration, the rate had reached 90 per cent.

Despite the tax avoidance devices that were employed, there is little question that these tax measures resulted in greatly reduced disposable income of the estate owners. Amory relates the experience of one millionaire who gave a taxi cab driver a tip amounting to only 20¢. The cabby, observing that the finely clothed man was obviously wealthy, complained of this. The rider reacted by offering to take back the tip, exclaiming, "that's $2.00 to me, man."[8] This story illustrates that in order to cover estate expenses after the owner's income became so heavily taxed, a good deal more of his gross earnings had to be allocated for this purpose.

From the preceding discussion of personal incomes of the very wealthy, it is reasonable to assume that the economic standing of estate people has weakened with their generally declining disposable incomes. It is now necessary to turn to the other dimension of economic strength, the wealth accumulations or fortunes in the possession of the rich.

FORTUNES

Though the present discussion of fortunes is especially concerned with the fortunes of families who inhabited North Shore estates, the money reserves of wealthy families in general will be considered. If the analysis was confined to the North Shore wealthy, whatever conclusions made about the economic burden of estate ownership would be limited to this group.

The huge American fortunes, many amounting to hundreds of millions of dollars, were typically made in the latter part of the 19th century. This was the time of dramatic industrial expansion and ruthless competition without government interference. It was during this period that opportunities for massive wealth accumulation were present. When at the end of the century the government began to intervene in business operations and place restrictions on corporate affairs, this era in American history ended. The great fortunes, however, remained.

The fate of these fortunes has been treated by several authors. Many of these huge accumulations, they have found, have been fragmented over the years, while only a handful have remained intact. Case histories of individual family fortunes have been undertaken, some of which will be referred to. Studies of a broader nature, however, are difficult to find. One of these few studies of fortunes in general was undertaken by Robert Lampman and is presented in his book, *The Share of the Top Wealth-Holders in National Wealth*. His major finding is that a declining concentration of wealth has taken place in America. The fortunes of the rich have become increasingly less substantial. [9]

There appear to be two sets of factors responsible for the reduction of family fortunes. The first of these is the characteristics of families and marriages of the wealthy. In the previous chapter these characteristics were considered. One of the findings was that a relatively high divorce rate seems to have existed among the very rich. This has had consequences for family fortunes. Each time a fortune possessor marries, the partner is legally entitled to a portion of the wealth. It is easy to see how just two or three marriages can substantially reduce a fortune. There are numerous examples of how, at the time of divorce, the less affluent partner received a settlement amounting to several million dollars. Such illustrations are provided by Tebbel. After presenting them, he states his view that dwindling fortunes are very much due to the "high cost of numerous divorces." [10]

Related to this marital factor is the affect of numerous offspring on the status of fortunes. The very rich, it has been observed, show a tendency to have more than an average number of children. Even if this were not the case and a normal number of children were present, there would still be heirs. In the absence of primogeniture and entail in this country, family fortunes have traditionally been divided among all of the children. This situation, especially where many children are present, contributes to the break-up of concentrations of wealth.

The case of the Thomas F. Ryan fortune is typical. Upon Thomas Ryan's death in 1928, his wealth was carved up into fifty-four equal amounts. Just twelve of these went to his wife. [11] It is because of numerous occurrences of this type that Tebbel partly explains the reduction of fortunes by referring to the "multiplication of heirs." Tebbel also considers the fate of fortunes that were left to one or two heirs. He finds that although this inheritance situation is necessary for keeping fortunes unfragmented, it does not insure that they will remain intact for long. Many inheritors, Tebbel finds, have not been concerned with conserving or even in managing fortunes with any degree of responsibility.

Fortunes have thus undergone reduction through conditions which were neither intended nor anticipated to have this result. But there were other conditions that were very obviously planned to reduce fortunes, planned by the adversaries of the very wealthy. These conditions were brought about by tax measures which were designed to curtail the handing down of huge fortunes.

Though the graduated inheritance tax was introduced before the thirties, it was not until this decade that the rate was made high enough to significantly cut into fortunes. There are cases of substantial portions of very large wealth accumulation going to the federal government upon the death of the holder. Such amounts might be as high as a few million dollars. When Murry Guggenheim died in 1939, the inheritance tax on his fortune was $3,449,000. This was the largest amount ever paid up to that time.   More recently, in 1956, Marshall Field left $150,000,000 upon his death and 80 per cent of this was reportedly pre-empted by taxes.

In addition to the direct influence the inheritance tax has had in reducing fortunes during inter-generational transfer, it has also had an indirect influence on fortune dissolution. It is clear that holders of large fortunes are preoccupied with the thought of leaving as little of their wealth to the government as possible upon their death. Given the progressive character of the inheritance tax, this goal is best accomplished when one bequeathes his money to a large number of beneficiaries. The tax, therefore, discourages passing fortunes down in one lump sum. Stated in a different way, the graduated inheritance tax encourages diffusing wealth among many heirs.

There is a side note to the subject of inheritance which is quite relevant. This is the fact that heirs, upon receiving the fortunes, may obtain tax abatements by giving away inherited possessions to non-profit organizations. Some individuals who inherited both a large fortune and a North Shore estate used this option to what they felt to be their advantage. They gave the estate away. In this way they were able to have the inheritance tax they were scheduled to pay reduced by the appraised value of the estate. Since the appraisals were generally higher than the estates could have been sold for, this was considered a once-in-a-lifetime opportunity to very profitably dispose of the estate.

Our central theme in this section has been that large wealth concentrations of both the rich on the North Shore and beyond, have been generally reduced since their accumulation. The lowering of this dimension of economic standing has meant that the ability to cope with the ever-growing expenses of owning a North Shore estate has lessened. It is the assumption in making this statement that incomes have not always been sufficient to meet these costs. There is evidence that the trend of increasingly lower disposable incomes of the very wealthy has made this more and more the case. With a simultaneous lowering of family fortunes to be used to help finance the operation of an estate, such luxury residences became economically more difficult, if not impossible, to maintain.

THE PREMIUM ON ESTATE LAND

In addition to the several economic conditions discussed which have acted to reduce the economic feasibility of owning a North Shore estate, there is another economic development that should receive some attention. This is the trend, intense since the end of the Second World War, of greater amounts of money being paid for vacant land on Long Island, especially tracts located in its western end in the vicinity of the estate area. The suburbanization movement has been responsible for these increasing land values. This building boom has created a great demand for home sites. As parcels of land have been bought up, remaining tracts have commanded higher and higher prices. This has acted as an incentive for many estate owners to sell their holdings. The individuals who sell their estates are usually influenced by more than this condition. They have typically seen first hand the increasing social and economic detractions of owning an estate.

To illustrate how substantially land values have increased, sales of comparable properties at various times may be considered. Leon Rushmore owned a large tract of land which was partly in Roslyn and partly in Old Westbury. Much of this property was inherited by him. He added to his land holding in 1935 when he purchased land at $300 an acre. When he sold most of his land in 1949 to a home developer he received $3,000 an acre. Recently, he disposed of a small tract he had retained. The price he obtained was $35,000 an acre. Rushmore's land was particularly valuable because it was very leniently zoned. Four houses to an acre was the zoning of a large portion of it.

Even the value of land with more restrictive zoning has gone up dramatically. Meyer Baker, a land appraisal expert working on the North Shore since 1919, notes that as late as 1940 a two-acre building plot in an estate area could be bought for under $1,000. Now such a plot commonly goes for above $20,000.

When it is considered how many plots are contained on an estate of several hundred acres, it can be realized what huge sums of money these holdings are worth. Estate acreage usually sells best if the estate is a large-size one. The builder knows that, in putting in roads and other improvements necessary for a development, the more houses he can build on the land, the more the cost of these land improvements can be distributed. This enables him to sell his house at a lower price. Though smaller estates are less attractive to developers, even these are now coming to be purchased by them for very large sums. The C. W. Thayer estate of twenty-one acres in Sands Point was recently sold for $175,000. Though this small estate has a few old structures on it, builders considering it were interested almost exclusively in the land.

Because of this economic fact of high value of estate land, many North Shore estate owners, especially short-time owners who have inherited the estates, have decided to sell. These decisions are made after the sellers weigh the advantages against the disadvantages of remaining in possession of the estate. Among the disadvantages is that of keeping a large sum of money, the market value of the estate, in a non-liquid state. The cash alternative is desired by many.

9

Personal Adjustment and Property Ownership

*There is only one success — to be able to spend
your life in your own way.*

Christopher Morley

In looking at the life cycle of several North Shore estates, one can see that a great many places were sold directly after the death of the original owners. This wide-spread practice may, at first, not seem unusual; however, more than social and economic conditions were responsible for this pattern. For, even as far back as the 1920's, a time when estates were very much socially desirable and economically feasible, this pattern could be observed. Several newspaper articles that appeared in the 1920's revealed that estates had currently been sold or left neglected upon the death of the men who built them. The heirs, it was noted, seemed merely to lack the desire to keep the place.

This pattern of estates being abandoned after their founders' demise is not characteristic of any single time period. It has occurred regularly over the last fifty years.

In view of this, it is necessary to go beyond social and economic conditions in the analysis of change on the North

151

Shore. For these conditions have been present only in certain time periods. They cannot, therefore, fully explain the pattern discovered.

To fill the gap in our interpretation, factors that are neither social, economic, nor political must be introduced. Such factors do exist. They are psychological factors and refer to the subjective-personal meaning of estates for the owners.

In bringing these additional factors into our interpretation of the decline of the Gold Coast, we will begin to deal formally with the psychology of estate ownership. This will involve a consideration of the basic motivations that often cause a person to seek or maintain an estate.

It will be maintained that there is often a difference in psychological state (or personality structure) between an estate's original owner and its inheritor. This difference manifests itself as a difference in the way an estate is valued. Because of one of two reasons to be discussed, the personal meaning of estate ownership is far greater for the original owner of an estate than it is for the person who later receives it as a legacy.

In the first of the two following discussions, it will be suggested that many of those people who built great estates on the North Shore may have had personality conflicts which caused them to display their wealth so flagrantly. This interpretation will view the establishment of an impressive estate as a compensatory mechanism used by those who felt they were lacking in some way.

The second discussion will consider the psychological dependence on estates that often grows out of prolonged estate ownership. When a strong emotional tie to an estate exists, there is little that can cause the owner to dispose of it.

STATUS ANXIETY

There is a motivational theory that may be used to understand why at least some of the wealthy people originally came to the North Shore and why they established estates there.

According to this theory, these estate founders were largely insecure people. The root of their insecurity was a marked apprehension about losing their positions as members of the upper class.

It does seem to be the case that most of the people who came to the North Shore when the Gold Coast was emerging were thought of as the new rich, the "nouveau riche." This designation applied to those wealthy individuals whose fortunes had a very brief history. Often their wealth had its origin in themselves. Their parents or grandparents were relatively poor and were members of the lower or middle class. There was a great deal of prejudice against the new rich on the part of the well-established upper class.

The extreme wealth of the "nouveau riche" was enough to gain them entry into the upper class. But their position there was not a very secure one. For although they had the prerequisite of money, they lacked many traditional upper-class characteristics — formal education, cultured mannerisms, and an upper-class family background. The weaknesses in their background may have made these persons apprehensive about their newly-gained social position, on the one hand, and unable to properly adjust to upper-class life, on the other.

This personal situation and the psychological consequences for those who shared it have been discussed by many theorists and writers. Milton Gordon has treated it under the subject of "stratification variables" which determine one's class position. Economic power and social status are identified as key variables of this type. If an individual or group such as the "nouveau riche" ranks high on one and low on another, "certain strains and pressures toward 'marginality' may come into being." By "marginality," Gordon means being on the border between two classes and not knowing in which class one belongs. He also uses the term "stratification inconsistency" to emphasize the precarious aspect of this situation. Gordon maintains that those exposed to marginality may experience psychological problems. These, in turn, can produce certain behavioral patterns. [1]

In accordance with this view, the behavioral pattern involving

material extravagance and ostentatious display is seen as a
neurotic reaction. Their obsessive spending of money resulted
from their desire to exhibit this single major upper-class attri-
bute: the possession of substantial wealth. This intense desire
was caused by the feeling of insecurity which they had about
their tenuous social standing.

The behavior of this group has been recorded by many observers. Josephson, in *The Robber Barons*, states: "Limited in
their capacity of enjoyment and bored, yet prompted to outdo
each other in prodigality, the New Rich experimented with ever
new patterns or devices of consumption." [2] Lundberg observes:
"Judged by the way they squander money on vapid amusement
and bizarre decoration, the rich are a psychopathic class...." [3]
F. Scott Fitzgerald lived among these people for awhile. Many
of his impressions are clearly set forth in his novel, *The Great
Gatsby*. [4] Gatsby himself is an important character to consider
for our purposes. The following description of him is provided
by the social scientist Harold Hages: "Gatsby was a sensitive
bootlegger who grew rich during prohibition—a poor boy who
made good financially but he was never certain of his success
in the field of social status; his opulent party giving and gran-
diose home represent the most adroit descriptions in American
literature of the anxiety-ridden parvenu on the make." [5]

A book was written by Mrs. John King Van Rensselaer in
the early 1920's entitled *The Social Ladder*. The author, herself
a member of the old-line upper class, obviously wrote the
book as a reaction to the extravagance and excess which she
had observed since the beginning of the century in areas such
as the North Shore. Her reaction to this was clearly negative.
She interpreted it as a brash attempt of the New Rich to reach
the top of the social scale where, according to Mrs. Rensselaer,
they had no right to be.

Her book essentially consists of an invidious comparison between the "society of wealth" (the New Rich) and the "society
of birth" (the Old Rich). Her belief is early stated that the
two "mingle no more readily than oil and water. Their present
apparent combination is merely a temporary emulsion brought

about by the rapid motion of the present. A few years of stability will disassociate them again, one rising, the other sinking, to its own level." [6] The author refers to the New Rich as "climbers." She maintains that the characteristics of this group "are cash rather than culture; arrogance rather than aristocracy." [7] Various estate areas are considered in her book. When the North Shore of Long Island is discussed, the claim is made that the so-called aristocracy here

> mostly bases its claim to that on money rather than lineage. Instead of using Burke's Peerage as a determinant of social acceptability, the Long Island imitator of the English gentleman is more likely to turn before forming his judgments to Dun and Bradstreet. To that part of the Long Island set, wealth and worth are interchangeable terms. Not a few of the leading spirits of the organization are removed from poverty and obscurity by a single generation. More than one had no American forebears whatever. [8]

The evidence that has been presented seems to indicate that the nouveau riche were very much conscious of their highly vulnerable social position, and that they strived to make this more secure by making their large fortunes as evident as possible. The ownership of a lavish estate was one of the means they employed.

If it is true that estates were sought out of feelings of insecurity (and inferiority), it may be asked why the children of these people who inherited and sold the estates were not similarly afflicted. A case can be made to show that this succeeding generation was granted a firmer place in the upper class, and, thus, it did not have to contend with the internal crisis faced by their parents.

The social position of this second generation was more secure for several reasons. First of all, they spent many of their early years in the environment of a boarding school with the sons and daughters of the old-line upper class. They were able in this way to become acquainted at an early age with upper-class life and learn its fundamentals. With this valuable background and with a good formal education by the time adulthood was reached, they were well equipped to make a complete adjustment and receive full recognition as members of the upper class. Unlike their parents, they felt no psychological need to "prove themselves" with an extravagant show of wealth. The family estate, therefore, lost its principal function when they inherited it. This may explain why their motivation to keep the family estate was relatively weak in contrast to that of their parents.

EMOTIONAL TIES TO ESTATES

There is a different, though compatible, psychological explanation for the pattern of individuals establishing North Shore estates and heirs disposing of them. This involves the strong emotional attachment which original or long-time owners of estates often have had for their residences. This attachment has been produced in two ways. Living on an estate for some time is the first source of emotional attachment to it. It is well known that long and close familiarity with any personal property can produce a deep concern for it and a strong desire to remain in possession of it.

The second basis for the attachment to estates is present where the owner is the estate's founder. It was seen in an earlier chapter that an estate is a custom-made commodity in every detail. In its creation the personal tastes and preferences of the owner are given maximum expression. It is not unlikely that estates were considered a reflection of oneself. This being the case, the basis for a strong emotional attachment is obvious.

Estate owners and close friends acknowledge that a genuine interest is often taken in the estate by its owner. This is considered to be especially true when the owner has been in possession of the estate since its beginning. One close observer of many of these people maintained that they "actually loved these places." This informant further relates that this attachment was often felt more strongly by either the husband or the wife.

It is claimed that the high sentiment for the estate was not shared by those who inherited it. As a consequence, they did not have an equally strong desire to remain in ownership of it. Why should they keep this custom-made residence! It was custom made for somebody else.

For the same reason, the estates when put on the market have little appeal to wealthy people who may even want to reside in an estate. It is the feeling of these people that they would rather spend more money and get exactly what they want. This usually means having a small estate built especially for them.

In a magazine article of 1948, a time when estates were being sold for a small portion of their original cost, the reader was informed that "there are bargains for sale, if you've got the chips and the inclination to settle for someone else's dream." [9]

An earlier article in a periodical designed for estate people treated this issue from a different perspective. The purpose of the article was to advise prospective creators of estates that it is important to plan for future re-sale when deciding on a plan and design for the present. A well-designed and planned estate will tend to attract buyers and will garner a higher sale price, providing it has a general appeal. The place should, therefore, be built with many conventional features so that it will be attractive to more than the original owner. The reader is finally advised that "it is well to avoid any eccentricities in plan or in appearance which would highly individualize the dwelling." [10]

It appears, in conclusion, that most of the estates were very personal possessions. Because of this, the original owners felt very close to them, while strangers and even offspring (many of whom had established their own separate residence before they came to inherit the parents' place) did not share this feeling. This explains why so many estates have been held by their founders with steadfast determination despite the decreasing social prestige and increasing economic burden of estate ownership only for the estates to become unwanted immediately after the owner's death.

PART THREE
Conclusion

10

Community Change: Process and Prospects

*The most incomprehensible thing about the world
is that it is comprehensible.*

Albert Einstein

The best prophet of the future is the past.

John Sherman

The story of Long Island's Gold Coast is a simple tale
laced with complexities. It is simple because anyone who has
lived on Long Island for some time, especially in the vicinity
of the North Shore, can relate the dramatic physical and social
change that has occurred in this upper-class area. He could
describe how most of the palatial residences have one-by-one
been converted by builders into subdivisions or transformed by
institutions into colleges, day schools, and homes for the deaf,
blind or aged. He could tell that the lavish parties at which
such notables as Enrico Caruso sang and Charles Lindbergh
or a future King of England danced and drank have disappeared
forever. Though the change is evident to many, the full set of
facts responsible for this change is extensive in number, complex
in nature, and often obscure.

When the author first became interested in the North Shore and as he began to review the written materials on the area, it soon became apparent that the existing literature provided little description and less understanding of the change that has occurred in this region. It appeared that a comprehensive study was needed which would both identify and illuminate this change. Such an analysis has been the goal of this book.

Discussed critically in the introductory chapter were the contributions made by several noted persons to the understanding of community change. The work of the economic determinists, of which the famous concentric zone theory of Burgess is an example, was first considered. It was argued that to rely entirely on economic factors to explain changing community characteristics, as these men tried to do, is a gross oversimplification. The analysis of central Boston performed by Firey was cited to show that purely social factors are also determinants of community change. The work of the more comprehensive theorist, F. Stuart Chapin, Jr., was then considered. Chapin postulated that physical change in areas is caused by the combined influence of social and economic, as well as political factors. Yet even this sweeping theoretic framework of Chapin was felt to be too narrow because instances of change were pointed to which appear to have taken place without the influence of any of these variables. These are explainable, it was maintained, only when reference is made to subjective-personal factors. Such factors are peculiar to the psychology of individual property owners. They are, so to speak, "psychological" factors. Only when a theoretic scheme takes all of these factors into account is a full understanding of community change possible. The present study of the North Shore of western Long Island attempted to utilize such a complete theoretic framework. In this way, it was hoped that the possibilities of this type of comprehensive approach for maximizing understanding of community change would be illustrated.

The overall thesis of this paper has therefore been that the change that has taken place on Long Island's North Shore has been caused by the collective influence of changing social, psychological, political, and economic conditions. By treating the North Shore as a case of community change, the author sought to provide evidence for his belief that the determinants or causes of such change are many both in number and variety.

The book was divided into three parts. Part I consisted of a historical and descriptive review of the North Shore. The purpose of this section was to provide a detailed picture of the change that has occurred on the North Shore over the last 70 years.

It was revealed in Part I that the principal period of estate development on the North Shore was the first two decades of this century. Throughout this period, America's wealthiest families came to the North Shore seeking to segregate themselves in the exclusive community that was emerging there. With 600 costly estates covering the entire area and dazzling affairs of high society commonplace, the name "Gold Coast" was applied to the North Shore.

The narrative continued by considering the dramatic change that has taken place on the North Shore. This has involved the reduction and fragmentation of the estate community. "The decline of the Gold Coast" was the phrase adopted to denote this pattern of change.

As far back as the mid-1920's signs that the estate community was beginning to deteriorate began to appear. At this time some of the few estates up for sale were being bought by people whose intentions were to transform the estates into other uses (e.g., housing developments or golf clubs). This now indicated that the demand for a lavish estate residence on the North Shore was falling.

This trend became increasingly stronger in the decades that followed. It persists today and, under existing conditions, can be expected to manifest itself until the estate community has dwindled to virtually nothing.

Though a large number of estates still can be found on the North Shore, these generally are smaller than and lack the expensive features of those that existed in the first quarter of the century. Moreover, the estates no longer exist one after the other in an unbroken sequence. Large tracts of land once part of the estate community are now used for non-estate purposes. This change is reflected in the type of social life now enjoyed by estate dwellers. As chapter IV revealed, the social life of today differs in several respects from that which existed when the estate community was intact. These changing features of North Shore land and life are what are referred to when the expression "the decline of the Gold Coast" is used.

Having described the growth and decline of the Gold Coast in Part I, Part II, the major section of the book, treated factors that appear to be responsible for the decline. Rather than developing an interpretation that emphasized either political, social, psychological, or economic factors, a multi-dimensional interpretation was aimed for which took all of these factors into account. The approach was to present and evaluate every important social fact that seems to be related to the decline of the Gold Coast, and to do this in a logical and, where possible, a chronological fashion.

A conclusion of that analysis is that community change on the North Shore cannot be explained merely in economic terms as' many have tried to do. Though changing economic conditions have certainly been involved, social, psychological, and political conditions were found to be important as well.

The decline, moreover, is related to both changing local and national conditions. The impact on the Gold Coast of change on each of these levels was considered.

Brought down to basics, the decline of the Gold Coast must be viewed as a phenomenon caused by members of a certain socio-economic group becoming less motivated to buy or retain a large estate on Long Island's North Shore. Such motivation has decreased because the social desirability and economic feasibility of owning an estate here has substantially lessened. Such a lessening has occurred principally because the estate people, with a lowering of their national and local political power, were unable to prevent it.

In the next few paragraphs the highlights of some of the

more significant findings of Part II will be presented. To begin this brief discussion, a few basic questions are posed. Why, over the years, did people who were able to build or maintain an estate on the North Shore become less motivated to do so? Indeed, did the economic standing of wealthy Americans become reduced to such an extent that they were no longer able to afford this?

As a result of the Great Depression, adverse government tax policies, and unfavorable upper-class marital and family characteristics, it apparently became both more difficult to accumulate wealth and virtually impossible to pass large fortunes intact onto succeeding generations. At the same time, establishing or maintaining a North Shore estate became an increasingly more expensive undertaking. Despite all this, however, it seems unquestionable that a large number of people able to afford the estates of the North Shore has continued to exist. It therefore appears that the desirability of a North Shore estate has become substantially reduced. Many things seem to be responsible for this. Owning an expensive estate, first of all, has lost much of its social significance. The fierce competition that once existed to live in a lavish country-type residence is no longer to be found among the upper class. The decreased importance of an estate as a status marker was held to be a function of the changing life style of the rich. The North Shore estate has particularly lost its attractiveness to wealthy individuals because of the changing character of Long Island. The image of Long Island has changed largely through the influence of the post-World War II suburbanization movement. Besides the declining prestige of owning a North Shore estate brought about by the changing Long Island scene, some practical disadvantages have inhered. With estates in close proximity to high-density, middle-class housing developments, estate owners began to experience frequent incidents of trespassing and vandalism.

Despite these and other undesirable aspects of owning a North Shore estate, a number of large estates continue to be maintained, some with as much care as when the Gold Coast flourished. Psychological factors were pointed to in explaining this. Some of the owners of the surviving estates were found to be emotionally attached to their places. This strong personal attachment results from living in estates, all of which are highly individualized, for long periods of time. The attachment is responsible for motivating these owners to live in the estates even in the face of mounting economic and social impracticality.

In addition to all of these changing circumstances, political conditions over the years were surveyed. It was found that the political power of North Shore estate dwellers, once very strong, deteriorated as time passed. This power had been used on the local level to preserve both the character of the North Shore and the nominal property taxes that were originally levied on estates. On the national level, the political influence served to prevent government policies harmful to the wealthy. In short, the political power of the estate owners was used to preserve their way of life. It was inevitable that, as their political position weakened, their ability to defend themselves became reduced.

Thus, a multitude of social, psychological, political, and economic circumstances have been responsible for the change that has been taking place on the North Shore. By considering the significance of these different types of phenomena, this study sought to illustrate the value of a multi-dimensional analysis.

It was pointed out on several occasions in the book that some of the factors considered, though they have influenced the decline of the Gold Coast, have not contributed to it in a direct way. These factors, which include most of the political conditions and some of the social conditions discussed, were responsible for bringing about other conditions which did have a direct bearing on the change that occurred on the North Shore. For example, the fact that founders of great American fortunes came to have a large number of decendants did not in itself directly contribute to the break-up of the North Shore estate community. But this social condition (the presence of numerous heirs) brought about the economic condition of the fragmentation of large fortunes. Because large family fortunes have sometimes been used to maintain an estate in lieu of sufficient incomes, this economic condition directly influenced the decline of the Gold Coast.

The factors considered in the paper can then be divided into two groups. Factors that appear to have directly contributed to the change on the North Shore would be labeled "primary," while those factors that have contributed indirectly could be called "secondary." These newly introduced terms are not used to imply the importance of one set of factors over another. Since it is impossible to imagine how the community change on the North Shore would have occurred in the absence of either set, both are considered equally important. The dichotomy has been developed merely to obtain a more precise picture of the causal relationship between the various factors identified and the North Shore community change.

Other one-time estate areas in the United States have shared the fate of the North Shore. This is understandable in the light of our finding that more than changing local conditions have been responsible for the reduction and fragmentation of the North Shore estate community. It would be interesting to see how closely the development of these other areas has paralleled that of the North Shore. Unfortunately, studies of these places, as inclusive as the one attempted here, do not exist.

Many rich Americans have been attracted to lands outside of the United States as locales for estates. These areas, which include Puerto Rico and sections of South America, have for the most part not been affected by the changing conditions which have made sections of this country, particularly the North Shore of Long Island, so unattractive for estates. The present-day travel possibilities with the jet plane have brought these foreign places very close to this country. Leaving from New York City, it takes only a few hours longer today to get to South America than it took fifty years ago to get to Cold

Spring Harbor.

Care has been taken in this discussion to claim no more than that the Gold Coast has declined. Its complete fall or disappearance has not taken place. Estates slowly continue to go down. But, though this movement may be slow, it is steady. Indications are that the passing of each year will continue to bring the passing of a few estates. It is conceivable that at some point in the not distant future an article will appear in the local newspapers entitled, "Long Island's Last Large Estate."

The remaining estate properties constitute the last large open tracts of land to be found in the densely populated western end of Long Island. Because of this, these parcels are in great demand. Though builders of residential subdivisions are especially anxious to acquire them, organizations both public and private are also interested. Large corporations, private and public schools, and religious groups are among the many active competitors for the remaining open tracts on the North Shore.

In addition to those who are interested in the remaining estates for development, there are others who are concerned with preserving as many of these holdings as possible. Some who have this concern are the estate owners themselves who would like to see their holdings maintained for posterity. Mrs. Alexandra E. McKay of Muttontown and Harry F. Guggenheim of Sands Point are among these owners. Mrs. McKay in 1964 gave Nassau County a permanent legal interest in her 95-acre estate and a limited right to use 58 acres of it through an "open space" easement. Future owners of the property will have to recognize this legal agreement which would prohibit them from developing the estate. Harry F. Guggenheim took steps in 1967 to insure the preservation of his 90-acre estate by announcing his intention to will it to Nassau County upon his death for use as a park.

In addition to the estate owners who would like to see the remaining estates survive, the new non-estate North Shore residents are also concerned with this. They see the estates as a major asset in enhancing the aesthetic qualities of their communities. The estates are also seen as a good source of tax revenue with few needs for government services.

Many agencies, both public and private, also are concerned with the future of North Shore estates. The Open Space Action Institute, a private, non-profit, staffed organization, is among these agencies. O.S.A.I. has attempted since its creation in 1964 to locate large private holdings in the New York Metropolitan area and advise the owners on possible methods of preserving their land beyond their lifetimes.

The Nassau County Planning Commission has taken an active role in fostering the non-development of choice North Shore land. It has given active assistance to village planning and zoning boards in solving their problems. The Commission has encouraged and guided conservation efforts such as in the picturesque area of Mill Neck Creek, where estate owners have relinquished development rights on their land to insure its preservation. This public agency has been further active by advocating the "cluster principle" in developing estates. The cluster approach involves the development of a portion of the property more intensely than permitted under the zoning and retaining the remaining area as permanent open land. While the overall density of development of the property is no different in this approach than in the conventional subdivision method, its important advantage is that of keeping prime land undeveloped.

The Nassau-Suffolk Regional Planning Board has also been concerned with the future of estates. As part of the Board's comprehensive planning program, a special planning study of the North Shore has been undertaken to determine the problems and prospects of this area. Out of this study, which included an attitude survey of North Shore residents, will come recommendations for special treatment of public projects on the North Shore to have maximum benefits for and minimum detrimental effects on the area.

It is appropriate that the eventual development of these lands be given careful consideration by the planning bodies on Long

Island. If they do not seek to influence this development, builders and often haphazard village zoning will continue to dictate it. Before too long, the discovery may be made that land to fill recreational, educational, or other institutional needs of the people of Long Island and the New York Metropolitan region no longer exists.

For planning bodies and others interested in the future of the North Shore, this book should have practical application. It has identified a land-use trend of a large region and has explained how it began and why it can be expected to continue. Equipped with some of the hypotheses that have been formulated, it is even possible to predict the approximate time and manner of disposition of an individual estate, given some clues to the economic and psychological situations of the owner.

The findings in this study can also be used in developing programs to implement planning recommendations for land presently used for estates. For example, it may be felt that it is important to preserve a part of the estate community. Such a recommendation might be justified on the grounds that the estates, viewed collectively as one type of residential area, provide a desirable residential balance in what would otherwise be a suburban region of highly standardized residential communities. Or the preservation of part of the estate community might be justified on purely aesthetic grounds, that estate properties consist of lands in very much their original state which any passerby can view and appreciate. If halting of change on the North Shore became an objective, what steps might the government take to achieve it?

Before treating this question it must be pointed out that some of the factors that have contributed to the reduction and fragmentation of the estate community are no longer operative. These factors, such as the changing image of Long Island, are essentially irreversible; they are no longer capable of being manipulated. A few factors, however, can still be controlled. The question is, therefore, which of these should be altered to achieve the goal of preserving what is left of the estate community?

A person who is of the belief, discredited in this study, that economic determinants alone lie behind the change that has occurred on the North Shore, might say that only if the ownership of estates is made more economically desirable can the decline of the Gold Coast be checked. He might suggest that subsidies be given by the government to owners of estates, either in the form of property-tax abatements or perhaps by making available government maintenance workers who could travel about from estate to estate and help to maintain them. In short, if one sees the problem of the decline of the Gold Coast as solely a function of economics, the solution would be an economic one.

This study has revealed, however, that more than economic conditions have been involved. To increase the economic feasibility of owning and operating estates, therefore, will not necessarily insure their continued existence. A more realistic approach would be to also strive to increase the social desirability of owning an estate. To do this, the government might seek to intensify law enforcement activities in estate areas. A special effort might be made to apprehend trespassers or vandals on estates. Stricter laws against trespassing might be considered. Another possible proposal would be to keep major public improvements in estate areas to a minimum. For example, a major public road might be planned for the periphery of an estate area, even though the most direct route is right through the middle of it. By these means, in conjunction with the economic measures previously noted, the ownership and operation of a North Shore estate can be made both more socially and economically attractive. If, then, the preservation of the estate community, or its disappearance for that matter, is the goal of the regional government, both the social and economic determinants of community change must be taken into account in formulating the means to achieve this objective.

This study, then, has some real policy implications. By explaining in depth the factors responsible for "the decline of the Gold Coast," it has attempted to provide the reader with a thorough understanding of this phenomenon. And it is generally agreed that before a phenomenon can be controlled, it must be understood.

But it is felt that the greatest value of this book does not lie in the direct application of its findings to influencing future change on the North Shore. Rather, it is hoped that the study will add to theory of community change by demonstrating that such change can best be understood from a broad, interdisciplinary perspective. If the value of this unconventional approach to understanding community change has been illustrated in this study, perhaps persons wishing to understand change in areas far removed from the North Shore will be attracted to use a similar approach.

Appendix

TABLE VI

POPULATION OF NORTH SHORE MUNICIPALITIES
1920-1965

	1920	*1930*	*1940*	*1950*	*1960*	*1965*
Counties						
Nassau	126,120	303,053	406,748	672,765	1,300,171	1,397,727
Suffolk	110,246	161,055	197,355	276,129	666,784	892,932*
Townships						
Hempstead	70,790	186,735	259,318	432,506	740,738	783,419
North Hempstead	26,370	62,202	83,385	142,613	219,088	234,505
Oyster Bay	20,296	36,869	42,594	66,930	290,055	325,755
Huntington	13,893	25,582	31,768	47,506	126,221	162,367*
Estate Villages**						
Asharoken	NA	98	48	116	253	390*
Bayville	NA	1,042	1,516	1,981	3,962	4,988
Brookville	NA	NA	204	337	1,468	2,601
Centre Island	NA	139	134	199	270	290
Cove Neck	NA	276	130	200	299	310
East Hills	NA	NA	343	2,547	7,184	8,441
Flower Hill	NA	NA	666	1,948	4,590	4,706
Huntington Bay	NA	357	408	585	1,267	1,496*
Kings Point	NA	1,294	1,247	2,445	5,410	5,826
Lake Success	NA	295	203	1,264	2,954	3,176
Lattingtown	NA	NA	613	745	1,461	1,631
Laurel Hollow	NA	161	110	169	834	1,176
Lloyd Harbor	NA	480	603	945	2,521	3,076*
Matinecock	NA	484	428	507	824	869
Mill Neck	NA	516	101	505	701	956
Muttontown	NA	NA	335	382	1,265	1,657
North Hills	NA	339	295	330	359	333
Old Brookville	NA	423	356	644	1,126	1,359
Old Westbury	NA	1,264	817	940	1,756	1,936
Oyster Bay Cove	NA	NA	466	561	988	1,188
Roslyn Harbor	NA	NA	233	316	925	1,129
Saddle Rock	71	74	69	33	1,109	1,032
Sands Point	284	438	628	860	2,161	2,447
Upper Brookville	NA	NA	456	469	1,045	1,181
City of Glen Cove	8,664	11,430	12,415	15,130	23,817	25,029

NA: Not Available

 * Estimated

** A few villages have undergone expansion since their incorporation. But, since the annexed areas were in all cases sparsely populated, the expansions did not significantly influence village population totals.

Sources: United States Bureau of the Census and Long Island Lighting Company

TABLE VII

ESTATE VILLAGES – DATES OF INCORPORATION AND TWENTY YEAR BUILDING ACTIVITY SUMMARY

Estate Village	Incorporation Date	Building Permits for Single Family Homes – 1946-1965
Asharoken	1925	NA
Bayville	1919	974
Brookville	1931	313
Centre Island	1926	81
Cove Neck	1927	37
East Hills	1931	1,758
Flower Hill	1931	1,004
Huntington Bay	1924	NA
Kings Point	1924	1,006
Lake Success	1927	715
Lattingtown	1931	366
Laurel Hollow	1926	234
Lloyd Harbor	1926	NA
Matinecock	1928	123
Mill Neck	1925	176
Muttontown	1931	207
North Hills	1929	41
Old Brookville	1929	192
Old Westbury	1924	395
Oyster Bay Cove	1931	178
Roslyn Harbor	1931	221
Saddle Rock	1911	233
Sands Point	1912	489
Upper Brookville	1932	220

NA – Not Available
Sources: Nassau County Planning Commission and villages listed above.

TABLE VIII

LAND USE OF ESTATE VILLAGES (IN ACRES) — 1966

Estate Village	Residential Development	Public Parks and Buildings	Institu- tions	Private Clubs	Other (Vacant, etc.)	Total area
Asharoken	210	0	0	0	330	540
Bayville	430	78	29	23	364	924
Brookville	1,718	239	129	20	581	2,687
Centre Island	391	2	0	14	299	706
Cove Neck	602	53	0	0	132	787
East Hills	894	66	31	2	457	1,450
Flower Hill	636	36	16	84	323	1,095
Huntington Bay	310	30	0	110	290	740
Kings Point	1,431	242	58	10	384	2,125
Lake Success	356	122	15	304	408	1,205
Lattingtown	1,367	101	126	250	639	2,483
Laurel Hollow	1,243	13	55	37	520	1,868
Lloyd Harbor	1,760	1,510	300	50	2,350	5,970
Matinecock	909	74	87	336	257	1,663
Mill Neck	1,183	13	83	0	383	1,662
Muttontown	2,713	20	0	197	969	3,899
North Hills	437	243	32	463	582	1,757
Old Brookville	1,474	1	37	237	788	2,537
Old Westbury	3,145	60	746	105	1,205	5,261
Oyster Bay Cove	1,820	12	41	0	784	2,657
Roslyn Harbor	504	0	2	134	112	752
Saddle Rock	122	10	0	0	37	169
Sands Point	1,365	312	29	378	659	2,743
Upper Brookville	1,435	24	329	187	803	2,778

Source: Adapted from *Existing Land Use* (Nassau-Suffolk Regional Planning Board, 1968) Table V, pp. 7-16.

TABLE IX

NORTH SHORE ESTATES OF 100 + ACRES
IN 1954 AND 1968

	1954	1968
Suffolk County	10	2
Nassau County	51	21
North Hempstead Township	14	5
Oyster Bay Township	37	16
North Shore (total)	61	23

TABLE X

PRESENT USE OF NASSAU COUNTY ESTATES
OF 100 + ACRES DEVELOPED SINCE 1954

Present Use	Number of Developed Estates
Housing Development	15-1/2
Private Golf Course	5-1/2
Smaller Estates	4
School	2-1/2
Public Park or Wildlife Sanctuary	2-1/2
Total	30

TABLE XI

SCHOOL TAX RATES* IN SELECTED
NORTH SHORE COMMUNITIES, 1943-1968

	1943	1948	1953	1958	1963	1968
Brookville	$ .28	$ .49	$1.11	$1.92	$4.89	$6.21**
Cove Neck	.72	1.35	1.54	2.82	5.07	7.45**
East Hills	1.27	2.07	3.30	5.59	7.15	9.94**
Jericho	.34	.60	.94	2.43	5.36	8.29**
Matinecock	.59	1.02	1.21	2.29	4.69	6.21**
Woodbury	.35	.69	2.05	4.03	5.82	8.51**

*per $100 assessed valuation
**proposed rate

Sources: School District 3 of North Hempstead, Central School Districts 2, 3, and 6 of Oyster Bay, School District 15 of Oyster Bay, and Nassau County Comptroller

References and Selective Bibliography

REFERENCES IN CHAPTER I

1. Dixon Wecter, *The Saga of American Society* (New York: Scribners 1937), p.11.
2. Reinhard Bendix and Seymour Martin Lipset, eds. *Class, Status and Power* (New York: The Free Press, 1966), p.116.
3. Dixon Wector, *The Saga of American Society*, p.22.
4. *Ibid.*, p.61.
5. *Ibid.*
6. C. Wright Mills, *The Power Elite* (New York: Oxford University Press, 1959), p.101.
7. Dixon Wecter, *The Saga of American Society*, p.141.
8. *Ibid.*, p.126.
9. Mrs. John King Van Rensselaer, *The Social Ladder* (New York: Henry Holt and Co., 1924), p.5.
10. C. Wright Mills, *The Power Elite*, p.54.
11. Dixon Wecter, *The Saga of American Society*, p.204.
12. C. Wright Mills, *The Power Elite*, p.55.
13. Dixon Wecter, *The Saga of American Society*, p.228.
14. Mary McLean (ed.), *Local Planning Administration* (Ann Arbor, Michigan: Cushing-Malloy, Inc., 1959), p.106.
15. Ernest W. Burgess, "The Growth of the City: An Introduction to a Research Project," in Robert E. Park, Ernest W. Burgess, and Roderick D. McKenzie (eds.), *The City* (Chicago: University of Chicago Press, 1925), p.47-62.
16. James M. Beshers, *Urban Social Structure* (New York: The Free Press of Glencoe, Inc., 1962), p.95.
17. Walter Firey, *Land Use in Central Boston* (Cambridge, Mass.: Harvard University Press, 1947), p.17.
18. *Ibid.*, p.19.
19. *Ibid.*
20. *Ibid.*, p.220.
21. *Ibid.*, p.130.
22. *Ibid.*, p.324.
23. F. Stuart Chapin, Jr., *Urban Land Use Planning* (New York: Harper and Brothers, 1957), p.69.
24. *Ibid.*, p.69.
25. *Time* (July 9, 1965), p.61.
26. *Ibid.*
27. *Ibid.*

REFERENCES IN CHAPTER II

1. The information on the Gardiner estate used in this discussion was obtained in an interview with Mr. Robert David Lion Gardiner on February 11, 1966. Mr. Gardiner is the present owner of the estate, now in its 16th generation of Gardiner ownership. For a brief history of the estate, see *Newsday* (August 2, 1947), p.14.

2. Quoted from a contemporary newspaper article by Roy W. Moger in *Roslyn — Then and Now* (Roslyn, N.Y.; Roslyn Public Schools, 1964), p.89.

3. Jacqueline M. Overton, *Long Island's Story* (Port Washington, N.Y.: I.J. Friedman, 1961).

4. The belief that E. D. Morgan was the first of the "Gold Coasters" to come to the North Shore was generally expressed in the interviews conducted by the author with persons long associated with and very much aware of the history of the Gold Coast. The author's research into assessment records revealed that some of the original estate structures which remain on the site of the Morgan estate were constructed in the 1880's.

5. Frederick Ruther, *Long Island To-day* (New York: The Essex Press, 1909), p.22.

6. Henry J. Lee, ed., *The Long Island Almanac and Year Book* (New York: Eagle Library Pub., 1931 & 1934).

7. The Long Island Almanac and Yearbook of 1930 expressed this popular belief. "Long Island has an unusually long growing season and is free from disastrous winds and floods." (P.79).

8. Leonidas Hubbard, Jr., "Country Homes on Long Island," *Outing* (December 1900).

9. Clara Brown Lyman, "How a Business Man Became a Skillful Country Gentleman," *The House Beautiful* (April 13, 1913), p.139.

10. Thorstein Veblen, *The Theory of the Leisure Class* (New York: Macmillan, 1899).

11. Long Island Rail Road, *Summer Homes on Long Island* (1904), p.10.

12. *The New York Herald* (December 1900).

13. This and other information on the Mackay estate was obtained from "the Donaldson Collection," an unpublished two-volume collection of annotated newspaper clippings, momentos, and other materials concerning the Mackay family. These volumes were found in the Roslyn Public Library.

14. Edward J. Smits, "Era of Elegance," *Herald Tribune* (April 11, 1965), p.10.

REFERENCES IN CHAPTER III

1. *World-Telegram* (October 20, 1942).

2. *Architectural Record* (December, 1904), p.532.

3. John Taylor Boyd, Jr., "The Residence of William R. Coe, Esquire," *Architectural Record* (March, 1921), p.224.

REFERENCES IN CHAPTER IV

1. The specific information on estates contained in this and succeeding paragraphs was obtained for the most part from tax assessment cards held by the Nassau County Assessment Department in Mineola, Long Island. These cards contain highly-detailed descriptions of all properties and buildings in Nassau County and often contain personal notes of the assessors who visited and described them.

2. *Manhasset Mail* (September 30, 1927), p.1
3. *Manhasset Mail* (August 24, 1928), p.1.
4. *Daily Review* (June 24, 1924), p.24.
5. These conclusions are based on information obtained from a number of sources including property ownership maps of the North Shore, tax assessment cards, and numerous persons interviewed who were close observers of land development during these two decades.
6. This comment was written in 1938 on the assessment card for the Evelyn Marshall Field estate.
7. Dorothy Inslee, "Otto H. Kahn" (typewritten, 1961).
8. *Cue* (March 3, 1942).
9. *World-Telegram* (October 20, 1942).
10. "North Shore," *Life,* 21 (July 22, 1946), p.73.
11. *World-Telegram* (December 29, 1939).
12. *Holiday* (1948).
13. "Life Goes to a Party," *Life* (October 4, 1948), p.162.
14. Tom Bernard, "Bargains in Dream Houses," *American Magazine* (October 1948), p.50.

REFERENCES IN CHAPTER V

1. Mrs. John King Van Rensselaer, *The Social Ladder* (New York: Henry Holt and Co., 1924), p.219.
2. *Herald Tribune* (February 1, 1963).
3. *Meadow Brook Club Book* (1924).
4. *Piping Rock Club Book* (1922).
5. Henry Isham Hazelton, *The Boroughs of Brooklyn & Queens, Counties of Nassau & Suffolk,* 2nd ed. (New York: Lewis Historical Pub. Co., Inc., 1925), p.931.
6. *The Long Islander* (July 2, 1926), p.1.
7. F. Scott Fitzgerald, *The Great Gatsby* (New York: Charles Scribner's Sons, 1925), p.39-41.
8. *The Long Islander* (July 23, 1926), p.1.
9. Based on records of building permits issued by the respective villages.
10. Jacqueline Overton, *Long Island's Story* (2nd ed.) With a sequel: *The Rest of the Story, 1929-1961,* by Bernice Marshall (Port Washington, N.Y.: I.J. Friedman, 1961), p.33.
11. Francis Wood, "High Society on Long Island Has Tired Blood," *Newsday* (July 15, 1963).

REFERENCES IN CHAPTER VI

1. Ferdinand Lundberg, *America's 60 Families* (New York: The Vanguard Press, 1937), p.292.
2. Matthew Josephson, *The Robber Barons* (New York: Harcourt, Brace, Inc., 1934), p.321.

3. Gustavus Myers, *The Ending of Hereditary American Fortunes* (New York: Julian Messner, Inc., 1939).
4. Matthew Josephson, *The Robber Barons*, p.338.
5. E. Digby Baltzell, *Philadelphia Gentlemen* (Illinois: The Free Press, 1958).
6. This and other information about Clarence Mackay was obtained from "the Donaldson Collection," an unpublished two-volume collection of annotated newspaper clippings, mementos, and other materials concerning the Mackay family. These volumes were found in the Roslyn Public Library.
7. Gustavus Myers, *The Ending of Hereditary American Fortunes*.
8. See discussions of the Long Island suburbanization movement in William M. Dobriner (ed.), *The Suburban Community* (New York: G.P. Putnam's Sons, 1958).
9. Ferdinand Lundberg, *America's 60 Families*, p.217.
10. "Parties and Bread Lines," *Literary Digest* (January 17, 1931), p.10.
11. *Nashville Tennessean* (January 1931).
12. Fireside Chat (September 30, 1944).
13. E. Digby Baltzell, *Philadelphia Gentlemen*.
14. "What Income Tax Figures Show," *Business Week* (December 15, 1934).
15. "Last Year's Millionaires," *Literary Digest* (December 22, 1934).
16. Nan and Ernest Pendrell, *How the Rich Live (and whom to tax)* (New York: Workers Library Pub., Inc., May 1939).
17. E. Digby Baltzell, *Philadelphia Gentlemen*, p.364.
18. Edward S. Corwin, and Jack W. Peltason, *Understanding The Constitution*, 3rd ed. (New York: Holt, Rinehart and Winston, Inc., 1964), p.162.
19. Robert J. Lampman, *The Share of Top Wealth-Holders in National Wealth 1922-56* (New Jersey: Princeton University Press, 1962).
20. Ferdinand Lundberg, *America's 60 Families*.
21. Information given by J.E. Aldred in a published interview. *World-Telegram* (October 20, 1942).
22. Ferdinand Lundberg, *America's 60 Families*, p.449.
23. Edward J. Smits, "Era of Elegance," *Herald Tribune* (April 11, 1965), p.10.
24. Roger Wines, "Vanderbilt's Motor Parkway: America's First Auto Road," *The Journal of Long Island History* (Fall 1962).
25. *History of Lake Success*. The name of the author and publication facts do not appear in this pamphlet. Circa 1949.
26. Cleveland Rodgers, *Robert Moses, Builder for Democracy* (New York: Henry Holt and Co., 1952), p.42.
27. *Ibid.*, p.44.
28. The Democratic Law Committee of Nassau County, *Wonderful Nassau Wants to Grow* (The Nassau County charter proposed by the Cuff Committee, 1932), p.IX.
29. Paul Bailey, ed., *Long Island* (New York: Lewis Historical Publishing Co., Inc., 1949), p.231.

REFERENCES IN CHAPTER VII

1. "Suburban Transportation Problems," (an address by Long Island Rail Road Vice President George Le Boutillier given before the Broadway Association on January 26, 1928).
2. "The End of the Long Island Rail Road as a Private Enterprise," *Long Island Forum* (November 1965), p.211.
3. Long Island Rail Road, *The Long Island Rail Road — Its Problems and Future* (September, 1942).
4. Long Island Rail Road, *What the Long Island Rail Road has Done and Plans to do to Improve Its Service* (answers to questions asked by the Public Service Commission and filed with the Commission on January 15, 1930).
5. This data on the Long Island Rail Road was obtained directly from Long Island Rail Road records which were made available through the Company's public relations office in Jamaica, New York.
6. William M. Dobriner, *The Suburban Community* (New York: G.P. Putnam's Sons, 1958), p.327.
7. *Ibid.*, p.329.
8. *Ibid.*
9. Jacqueline Overton, *Long Island's Story* (2nd ed.) With a sequel: *The Rest of the Story 1929-61*, by Bernice Marshall (Port Washington, N.Y.: I.J. Friedman, 1961), p.11.
10. Eric Larrabee, "The 6000 Houses that Levitt Built," *Harper* (September 1948), p.81.
11. Oscar G. Darlington, *Glimpses of Nassau County History*, (1949), p.2.
12. Eric Larrabee, "The 6000 Houses that Levitt Built," *Harpers* (1948), p.81.
13. *National Geographic* (March 1951).
14. Harvey W. Zorbaugh, *The Gold Coast and the Slum* (Chicago: The University of Chicago Press, 1929), p.63.
15. Cleveland Amory, *Who Killed Society?* (New York: Harper, 1960), p.524.
16. Thorstein Veblen, *Theory of the Leisure Class* (New York: Modern Library, 1934).
17. Cleveland Amory, *Who Killed Society?*, p.522.
18. C. Wright Mills, *White Collar* (New York: Oxford University Press, 1951).
19. This has been observed by Mills, Amory, Packard, Baltzell, and other contemporary theorists and social commentators. See selective bibliography.
20. *Newsday* (November 12, 1964).
21. It should be noted that this discussion concerns the uppermost economic strata of the upper class, that is, the wealthiest members of the upper class. There are some published empirical studies on divorce in the upper class in general. These show that divorce is no more prevalent in the upper class than in the lower classes. See Robert F. Winch, *The Modern Family* (New York: Holt, Rinehart and Winston, 1963), pp.706-708 for a listing and summarization of some of these studies. The fact is, however, that virtually no statistical analysis has been done of divorce among the millionaires and multi-millionaires who constitute the wealthiest sector of the upper class. The only study of these people that could be found was the Sorokin report

of 1925 (later cited). Though this study was done in 1925, it should not be considered outdated for use here. Rather, it is especially appropriate since, as chapter III revealed, the decline of the Gold Coast was initiated in the 1920s.

22. Cleveland Amory, *Who Killed Society?*
23. Pitirim Sorokin, "American Millionaires and Multi-millionaires," *The Journal of Social Forces*, III, No.4 (May 1925).
24. Ralph Thomlinson, *Population Dynamics* (New York: Random House, Inc., 1965), pp.177 and 182.

REFERENCES IN CHAPTER VIII

1. Bernice Marshall, *The Rest of the Story*, a sequel to Jacqueline Overton's *Long Islands Story* (Port Washington N.Y.: I.J. Friedman, 1961), p.14.
2. This figure was compiled from statistics in the Nassau County Planning Commission's *Twenty-Year Building Summary*, 1966.
3. *Long Island Trends* (a monthly socio-economic statistical newsletter published jointly by the Nassau and Suffolk County Planning Commissions).
4. William M. Dobriner, ed., *The Suburban Community* (New York: G.P. Putnam's Sons, 1958), p.193.
5. *World-Telegram* (October 20, 1942).
6. Ferdinand Lundberg, *America's 60 Families,* p.410.
7. "Vanishing Multi-Millionaires," *Literary Digest* (January 27, 1934).
8. Cleveland Amory, *Who Killed Society?* (New York: Harper, 1960).
9. Robert J. Lampman, *The Share of Top Wealth-Holders in National Wealth 1922-56* (New Jersey: Princeton University Press, 1962).
10. John Tebbel, *The Inheritors* (New York: G.P. Putnam's Sons, 1962), p.108.
11. *Ibid.*, p.141.
12. *Ibid.*, p.268.

REFERENCES IN CHAPTER IX

1. Milton M. Gordon, *Social Class in American Sociology* (Durham, N.C.: Duke University Press, 1958), p.237.
2. Matthew Josephson, *The Robber Barons* (New York: Harcourt, Brace, Inc., 1934), p.338.
3. Ferdinand Lundberg, *America's 60 Families* (New York: The Vanguard Press, 1937), p.409.
4. F. Scott Fitzgerald, *The Great Gatsby* (New York: Charles Scribner's Sons, 1925).
5. Harold M. Hages, Jr., *Social Stratification* (Cambridge, Mass: Schenkman Publishing Co., Inc., 1964), p.74.
6. Mrs. John King Van Rensselaer, *The Social Ladder* (New York: Henry Holt and Co., 1924), p.108.
7. *Ibid.*, p.239.
8. *Ibid.*, p.282.

9. Tom Bernard, "Bargains in Dream Houses," *American Magazine* (October 1948), p.50.

10. "Good Collateral When Needed," *Country Life in America* (March 1931), p.70.

SELECTIVE BIBLIOGRAPHY

BOOKS

Adrian, Charles R. *State and Local Governments.* 2nd edition. New York: McGraw-Hill Book Company, 1960.

Amory, Cleveland. *The Proper Bostonians.* New York: E.P. Dutton, 1947.

———. *The Last Resorts.* New York: The Universal Library, 1948.

———. *Who Killed Society?* New York: Harper, 1960.

Bailey, Paul. ed. *Long Island.* New York: Lewis Historical Publishing Co., Inc., 1949.

Baltzell, E. Digby. *Philadelphia Gentlemen.* Illinois: The Free Press, 1958.

———. *The Protestant Establishment.* New York: Ramdon House, 1964.

Bendix, Reinhard and Lipset, Seymour Martin (editors). *Class, Status and Power.* New York: The Free Press, 1966.

Bermingham, Stephen. *"Our Crowd": The Great Jewish Families of New York.* New York: Harper & Row, 1967.

Beshers, James M. *Urban Social Structure.* New York: The Free Press of Glencoe, Inc., 1962.

Blanchard, S. Fessenden. *Long Island Sound.* Princeton, N.J.: D. Van Nostrand Co., Inc., 1958.

Bollens, John C. *Special District Governments in the United States.* Berkeley, California: University of California Press, 1957.

Bollens, John C. and Schmandt, Henry J. *The Metropolis.* New York: Harper & Row, 1965.

Caldwell, Lynton K. *The Government and Administration of New York.* New York: Thomas Y. Crowell Co., 1954.

Chapin, F. Stuart, Jr. *Urban Land Use Planning.* New York: Harper and Brothers, 1957.

Chapin, F. Stuart, Jr. and Weiss, Shirly F. eds. *Urban Growth Dynamics.* New York: Wiley, 1962.

Corwin, Edward S. and Peltason, Jack W. *Understanding The Constitution.* 3rd ed.; New York: Holt, Rinehart and Winston, Inc., 1964.

Darlington, Oscar G. *Glimpses of Nassau County History.* 1949.

Dobriner, William M. *Class in Suburbia.* Englewood Cliff, N.J.: Prentice-Hall, 1963.

———. ed. *The Suburban Community.* New York: G.P. Putnam's Sons, 1958.

Firey, Walter. *Land Use in Central Boston.* Cambridge, Mass.: Harvard University Press, 1947.

———. *Man, Mind, and Land.* New York: The Free Press of Glencoe, 1960.

Fitzgerald, F. Scott. *The Great Gatsby.* New York: Charles Scribner's Sons, 1925.

Gabriel, Ralph Henry. *The Evolution of Long Island*. Port Washington, N.Y.: Ira J. Friedman, 1960.

Ginger, Ray. *Age of Excess — The United States from 1877-1914*. New York: The Macmillian Co., 1965.

Gordon, Milton M. *Social Class in American Sociology*. Durham, N.C.: Duke University Press, 1958.

Haar, Charles M. *Land-Use Planning: A Casebook on the Use, Misuse, and Re-use of Urban Land*. Boston: Little-Brown, 1959.

Hages, Harold M., Jr. *Social Stratification*. Cambridge, Mass.: Schenkman Publishing Co., Inc., 1964.

Handy, Rollo and Kurtz, Paul. *A Current Appraisal of the Behavioral Sciences*. Great Barrington, Massachusetts: Behavioral Research Council, 1964.

Hawley, Amos H. *The Changing Shape of Metropolitan America: Deconcentration Since 1920*. New York: Free Press, 1956.

Hazelton, Henry Isham. *The Boroughs of Brooklyn and Queens, Counties of Nassau and Suffolk*. 2nd ed.; New York: Lewis Historical Pub. Co., Inc., 1925.

Hicks, John D. *The American Nation*. 3rd ed.; Chambridge, Mass.: The River-side Press, 1955.

Josephson, Matthew. *The Robber Barons*. New York: Harcourt, Brace, Inc., 1934.

Lampman, Robert J. *The Share of Top Wealth-Holders in National Wealth 1922-56*. New Jersey: Princeton University Press, 1962.

Lee, Henry J. ed. *The Long Island Almanac and Year Book*. New York: Eagle Library Publications, 1931, and 1934.

Le Gallienne, Richard. *Vanishing Roads and Other Essays*. New York: G.P. Putnam's Sons, 1915.

Long Island Chamber of Commerce. *Long Island: The Sunrise Homeland*. 1930.

Lundberg, Ferdinand. *America's 60 Families*. New York: The Vanguard Press, 1937.

Manley, Seon. *Long Island Discovery*. New York: Doubleday, 1966.

McLean, Mary. ed. *Local Planning Administration*. Ann Arbor, Michigan: Cushing-Malloy, Inc., 1959.

Mills, C. Wright. *The Power Elite*. New York: Oxford University Press, 1959.

——. *White Collar*. New York: Oxford University Press, 1951.

Moses, Robert. *Working for the People*. New York: Harper and Brothers, 1956.

Myers, Gustavus. *The Ending of Hereditary American Fortunes*. New York: Julian Messner, Inc., 1939.

——. *History of the Great American Fortunes*. New York: Random House, Inc., 1910.

Overton, Jacqueline Marion. *Long Island's Story* (2nd ed.) With a sequel: *The Rest of the Story 1929-61*, by Bernice Marshall. Port Washington, New York: I.J. Friedman, 1961.

Packard, Vance. *The Status Seekers*. New York: David McKay Co., Inc., 1959.

Park, Robert E., Burgess, Ernest W., and Mckenzie, Roderick D. eds. *The City*. Chicago: University of Chicago Press, 1925.

Pendrell, Nan and Ernest. *How the Rich Live (and whom to tax)*. New York: Workers Library Publishers, Inc., May 1939.

Rodgers, Cleveland. *Robert Moses, Builder for Democracy.* New York: Henry Holt and Company, 1952.
Ruther, Frederick. *Long Island To-day.* New York: The Essex Press, 1909.
Shannon, Jasper B. *Money and Politics.* New York: Random House, Inc., 1959.
Spectorsky, August C. *The Exurbanites.* New York: Lippincott, 1955.
Tebbel, John. *The Inheritors.* New York: G.P. Putnam's Sons, 1962.
Thomas, Samuel F. *Nassau County: Its Governments and Their Expenditure Patterns.* New York: New York City College Press, 1960.
Thomlinson, Ralph. *Population Dynamics.* New York: Random House, Inc., 1965.
Van Rensselaer, Mrs. John King. *The Social Ladder.* New York: Henry Holt and Co., 1924.
Veblen, Thorstein. *Theory of the Leisure Class.* New York: Modern Library, 1934.
Wecter, Dixon. *The Saga of American Society.* New York: Scribner's, 1937.
Willhelm, Sidney M. *Urban Zoning and Land Use Theory.* New York: The Free Press of Glencoe, 1962.
Winch, Robert F. *The Modern Family.* New York: Holt, Rinehard and Winston, 1963.
Wood, Robert C. *Suburbia: Its People and Their Politics.* Boston: Houghton Mifflin, 1959.
Zorbaugh, Harvey W. *The Gold Coast and the Slum.* Chicago: The University of Chicago Press, 1929.

OTHER MATERIALS

Architectural Record. (December 1904).
Bernard, Tom. "Bargains in Dream Houses," *American Magazine,* (October 1948).
Boyd, John Taylor, Jr. "The Residence of William R. Coe, Esquire." *Architectural Record.* (March 1921), pp.195-224.
"Country House Construction Trends." *Architectural Record.* (November 1931), p.60.
Country Life In America (August 1908).
The Democratic Law Committee of Nassau County. *Wonderful Nassau Wants to Grow.* The Nassau County Charter proposed by the Cuff committee, 1932.
The Donaldson Collection. Two volumes of annotated newspaper clippings regarding the Mackay family. Held by the Bryant Library, Roslyn.
"The End of the Long Island Rail Road as a Private Enterprise," *L.I. Forum vol. XXVIII,* no.11, (November 1965).
Flynn, John T. "The Dwindling Dynasties," *North American Review,* (December 1930).
Fordyce, Dorothy M. *Your Local Government and How it Works.* A booklet of political information prepared for the Non-Partisan Civic Association, Inc.
"Good Collateral When Needed," *Country Life in America* (March 1931).
Great Neck Circle. vol. 1, no. 1, October 1950.
History of Lake Success. The name of the author and publication facts do not appear in this pamphlet. Circa 1949.

Hubbard, Leonidas, Jr. "Country Homes on Long Island," *Outing* (December 1900).

Inslee, Dorothy. "Otto H. Kahn." 1961. (typewritten).

Irwin, Francis. "Historical Oyster Bay." 1926. (mimeographed).

Larrabee, Eric. "The 6000 Houses that Levitt Built," *Harper* (September 1948), pp.79-88.

"Last Year's Millionaires," *Literary Digest* (December 22, 1934).

"Life Goes to a Party," *Life*. (October 4, 1948), pp.162-4.

The Long Island Association. *Know Long Island.* 1960.

Long Island Rail Road. *The Long Island Rail Road — Its Problems and Future.* September, 1942.

Long Island Rail Road. *Long Island Resorts.* 1911.

Long Island Rail Road. *What the Long Island Rail Road has Done and Plans to do to Improve Its Service.* (answers to questions asked by the Public Service Commission and filed with the Commission on January 15, 1930.)

Long Island Trends. (a monthly socio-economic statistical newsletter published jointly by the Nassau and Suffolk County Planning Commissions.)

Lyman, Clara Brown. "How a Business Man Became a Skillful Country Gentleman," *The House Beautiful* (April 13, 1913).

Nassau County Planning Commission. *Aspects* (a seven-part analysis of social, economic, and housing characteristics of Nassau County, N.Y.). 1962, 1963.

——. *Parks and Recreation.* August, 1964.

Nassau County Transit Commission. *Long Island Rail Road.* June 16, 1949.

Nassau-Suffolk Regional Planning Board. *Long Island Land Use — 1966.* March 1968.

National Geographic. March 1951.

"North Shore," *Life.* (July 22, 1946) pp.73-83.

Open Space Action Committee. *Stewardship.* 1965.

Parker, Maude. "Where are the Idle Rich." *The Saturday Evening Post.* (November 23, 1929).

"Parties and Bread Lines," *Literary Digest* (January 17, 1931).

Philips, Charles. "More or Less Abandoned Estates of Long Island," *New York Times* (August 13, 1922).

Prince, C. Matlack. "A Resort Country House on Long Island — the Garver Residence at Oyster Bay." *Architectural Record.* (March 1914), p.181.

Ransom, Charles E. (an unpublished and untitled six-page typewritten article written circa 1952).

——. (an unpublished, untitled, and undated seven-page typewritten article).

Schermerhorn, Richard, Jr. *Master Plan of the Great Neck District.* A regional study prepared for the Great Neck Association. 1927.

"Sculpture in a Long Island Estate." *Arts and Decoration.* (July 1925), p.28.

Smith, Louise Carter. "Long Island Motor Parkway." *Nassau County Historical Journal.* (Spring 1961).

Smits, Edward J. "Era of Elegance" *Herald Tribune* (April 11, 1965).

Sorokin, Pitirim. "American Millionaires and Multi-millionaires," *The Journal of Social Forces,* III, No. 4, (May 1925).

"Vanishing Multi-Millionaires," *Literary Digest* (January 27, 1934).
"What Income Tax Figures Show," *Business Week* (December 15, 1934).
Wines, Roger. "Vanderbilt's Motor Parkway: America's First Auto Road,"
    The Journal of Long Island History (Fall 1962).

Index

Index

REFERENCE - - NOT TO BE
TAKEN FROM THIS ROOM

WITHDRAWN

LONGWOOD PUBLIC LIBRARY
Middle Country Road
Middle Island, NY 11953
(631) 924-6400

LIBRARY HOURS

Monday-Friday	9:30 a.m. - 9:00 p.m.
Saturday	9:30 a.m. - 5:00 p.m.
Sunday (Sept-June)	1:00 p.m. - 5:00 p.m.